THEOGONY

The Library of Liberal Arts
OSKAR PIEST, FOUNDER

THEOGONY

HESIOD

Translated, with an introduction, by
NORMAN O. BROWN

. . . .

The Library of Liberal Arts
published by

Macmillan Publishing Company
New York
Collier Macmillan Publishers
London

Macmillan Publishing Company
866 Third Avenue
New York, New York, 10022
Collier Macmillan Canada, Inc.

First Edition
PRINTING   32 33 34 35   YEAR   9 0 1 2 3 4 5

Library of Congress Catalog Card Number: 53-4359
ISBN 0-02-315310-5

CONTENTS

INTRODUCTION

I. THE STRUCTURE OF THE *THEOGONY*

The charm of classical mythology, which has won so many readers for Ovid's *Metamorphoses*, has failed to save Hesiod's *Theogony* from neglect. The general reader of the *Theogony*, while admiring individual episodes, such as the story of Prometheus, cannot find a coherent purpose or unified structure in the poem as a whole; large tracts of the poem—the genealogical catalogues—seem to be inspired by no purpose higher than a dull encyclopedism. For proper appreciation of the *Theogony* the general reader needs the help of the scholar.

The task of the scholar is complicated by the fact that the text which has come down to us contains extensive interpolations which were inserted at a time so close to Hesiod's as to make them almost indistinguishable from Hesiod's own work. As a result the problem of the structure of the poem is inextricably interwoven with the problem of establishing the original text; the structure is an attribute of the original poem. For a hundred years scholars have been working on this problem without arriving at a text which commands general acceptance.[1]

In view of the complicated interrelation between the problem of the structure and the problem of the text, and in view of the disagreements among the experts, a fresh appraisal of the contents of the *Theogony* had best start with the obvious and the indisputable. At least one basic element in the plan of the *Theogony* seems to be obvious and indisputable—namely, to trace the history of the divine government of the universe from the first patriarch Sky (Uranus) through his son Cronus, the head of the Titans, to its culmination in the reign of Zeus the son of Cronus and head of the Olympian gods. This assumption is necessary in order to explain some of

---

[1] See Selected Bibliography, p. 49.

the narrative episodes which are clearly high lights of the poem, and which are admitted by all experts to be authentic parts of the original structure. These are (1) the castration of Sky by his son Cronus, instigated by his mother Earth (lines 154-210); (2) Zeus' escape from being swallowed by his father Cronus (lines 453-500); (3) the victorious battle of Zeus and the Olympian gods against the Titans (lines 617-735).

Once it is agreed that Hesiod's plan at least includes the history of the divine government of the universe up to its culmination in the monarchy of Zeus, then some other episodes can be seen to be integrally related to this main theme. Zeus' monarchy is consolidated by a tremendous exhibition of power in the battle against the Titans; this power is primarily manifested in the lightning bolts which are manufactured for Zeus by the Cyclopes, and in the strength of the Hundred-Arms who fight on the side of the Olympians. Hence the story of the birth of the Cyclopes and the Hundred-Arms (lines 139-153) and of their release from imprisonment by Zeus and consequent alliance with Zeus (lines 501-06; 617-28) are necessary parts of Hesiod's plan. For the same reason the story of how Styx, though one of the Titans, deserted to the side of Zeus along with her children—Glory, Victory, Power, and Strength—(lines 383-403), is related to the main theme: like the stories of the Cyclopes and the Hundred-Arms, it shows how Zeus' power is consolidated by judicious alliances with older divinities.

For a slightly different reason it is legitimate to say that Hesiod's plan requires the inclusion of some description of Zeus' children after the god's victory is attained. Creative energy is a fundamental attribute of power, and, in Hesiod's myth-language, is manifested in procreation; likewise, in Hesiod's myth-language, the character of a divine power is revealed in his children. For these reasons some description of Zeus' children, such as our text has in lines 886-end, is necessary after the battle against the Titans, and forms a fitting ending to the poem.

Thus one basic theme of the *Theogony* is the nature of the divine cosmos. The *Theogony* is planned to show the nature of the divine cosmos under two different aspects: the historical process culminating in Zeus' supremacy over the divine cosmos, and the character of Zeus' rule. But important as this theme is—indeed it has been called the backbone of the structure of the poem [2]—it does not account for large areas of the text which are universally agreed to be authentic parts of the original poem. Here we face the crucial dilemma in the solution of the interrelated problems of the text and the structure of the *Theogony:* either we must find additional themes which are part of the basic structural plan, or we must admit that the *Theogony* is in large part a structureless mess.

If the dilemma is faced, I do not think that there is any difficulty in naming additional themes which must be included in any inventory of the contents of the *Theogony.*

In the first place, it is obvious that Hesiod's plan covers not only the divine cosmos, but also the physical cosmos, and that the two are in his view so interrelated that it is not possible to treat the one without treating the other. Immediately after his introductory prelude (lines 1-115) Hesiod deals with the fundamental elements of the physical cosmos—Void; Earth; Void's children, Darkness, Night, Light, and Day; and Earth's children, Mountains, Sea, and Sky (lines 116-132); Hesiod also includes the cosmic force of Desire. From one or another of these primal elements of the physical cosmos—which are themselves divine powers—every other power mentioned in the *Theogony,* whether physical or non-physical, is descended. Hesiod then returns to the subject of the physical cosmos in a later part of the poem: a number of the first offspring produced by Earth and Sky, the Titans (lines 133-38), produce children who are further elements of the physical cosmos and who complete the picture of it. Ocean and Tethys produce the rivers and river nymphs (lines 337-70); Hyperion and Thea produce Sun, Moon, and Dawn (lines 371-74); Crius the father of Astraeus unites with Dawn to produce the winds and the stars (lines 375-82). All of these passages are universally

---

[2] Solmsen, *Hesiod and Aeschylus,* 20.

accepted as authentic parts of the original poem, and Hesiod, who is selective rather than encyclopedic in his treatment of Greek mythology, would not have included them unless it was part of his plan to cover the physical cosmos as well as the divine cosmos.

In the second place, it is obvious that Hesiod's plan covers not only the divine and the physical cosmos, but also the human cosmos. Otherwise there would not be included such unquestionably authentic passages as the elaborate genealogies of Night and Sea (lines 211-336). Hesiod gives as the children of Night a long list of personifications—Death and Strife, for example—which represent destructive forces at work in the human cosmos (lines 211-32). In juxtaposition and sharp contrast with the children of Night comes a long list of the daughters of Nereus, the eldest son of Sea; the Nereids are beneficent powers in the human cosmos (lines 233-64). The descendants of the other children of Sea (Thaumas, Phorcys and Ceto) represent marvels and monsters active in the human cosmos (lines 265-336).

The same concern with the human cosmos underlies another outstanding passage in the *Theogony*—the story of Prometheus (lines 506-616). Although the story of Prometheus' battle of wits against Zeus does exhibit Zeus' pre-eminence in wisdom and power, and hence does fit in with the primary theme of Zeus' control over the divine cosmos, yet major emphasis is placed on fateful consequences for mankind—the curse of womankind accompanies the blessing of fire. Similarly, in the concluding section of the *Theogony* where we find the enumeration of the children of Zeus (lines 886-955), the theme of the character of Zeus' rule is combined with the theme of the nature of the human cosmos; the emphasis is here placed on those children of Zeus who illustrate their father's dispensation to mankind.

The same concern with the human cosmos underlies two sections that have been rejected as interpolations by some critics, but which I believe to be integral parts of the basic thematic pattern of the *Theogony*. The first is the long passage in praise of Hecate (lines 404-52). Hecate is one of the older gods for whom Zeus finds an honorable place in his new order: in this respect the passage illustrates Zeus' re-organization of the divine cosmos. But the function assigned to Hecate by Zeus is that of being the great and beneficent intermediary between the divine cosmos and mankind: in this respect the passage is a vital part of the picture of the human cosmos under the dispensation of Zeus. The other passage is the description of the underworld region of Tartarus where Zeus imprisoned the defeated Titans (lines 736-819). The passage does contain repetitions and irrelevancies which must be regarded as interpolations. But the core is a description of the realm of Night and of the function of Night and her chief offspring, Death and Sleep, in the human cosmos. Given Hesiod's emphasis on Night and her progeny (lines 211-32), and given Hesiod's systematic concern with showing how Zeus integrates older powers into his new order, it is not too much to say that, to complete the picture of the physical cosmos and the human cosmos in Zeus' new order, this return to the subject of Night is necessary.

This inventory of the contents of the *Theogony* is enough to show that Hesiod has a theme that is complete in itself, and composed of interrelated parts: the divine, the physical, and the human cosmos. The same theme, in the same three aspects, is stated in the introductory invocation of the Muses (lines 1-114). Here we find not only a preliminary list of some of the leading figures in the divine and physical cosmos (lines 11-20), with emphasis on the sovereignty of Zeus (lines 47-49, 71-74), but also a picture of the role of the Muses in the human cosmos (lines 22-34, 75-103), and a promise to "tell how in the beginning the gods and the earth came into being, as well as the rivers, the limitless sea with its raging surges, the shining stars, and the broad sky above" (lines 105-110).

To understand a poem, it is not sufficient to state the theme; it is also necessary to discover the principle of organization according to which the parts are distributed throughout the whole, and which therefore gives structure and meaning to the whole. The difficulty with the *Theogony* is, of course, that structural analysis depends on establishment of the text, and *vice versa*. Since our definition of the theme is comprehensive and in itself excludes nothing, the principle of proceeding from the known to the unknown requires that we analyze the text of the *Theogony* as it is, subtracting only those parts which can with certainty be regarded as interpolations. There is in fact only one major episode which the experts agree to be an interpolation [3]—the account of the monster Typhoeus which challenged the supremacy of Zeus (lines 820-880). If we then eliminate the Typhoeus episode and simply take an inventory of the contents of the *Theogony*, in the light of our definition of the theme, we obtain the following table:

Section Number	Line Reference	Mythological Topic	Cosmic Theme		
I	1-115	Invocation of the Muses	Divine	Human	
II	116-153	Void, Earth; Sky, Mountains, Sea; Titans, Cyclopes, Hundred-Arms	Divine		Physical
III	154-210	Cronus castrates Sky	Divine		
IV	211-336	Curses of Night, blessings of Nereids; marvels and monsters of Sea		Human	
V	337-382	Rivers, Sun, Moon, Dawn, Winds, Stars			Physical
VI	383-403	Zeus' alliance with Styx	Divine		
VII	404-452	Zeus, Hecate, and mankind	Divine	Human	
VIII	453-506	Zeus' conflict with Cronus (first phase)	Divine		
IX	507-616	Zeus, Prometheus, and mankind	Divine	Human	
X	617-735	Zeus' conflict with Cronus (final phase)	Divine		
XI	736-819	Tartarus and realm of Night		Human	Physical
XII	881-1022	Zeus' monarchy and offspring	Divine	Human	

---

[3] Cf. *ibid.*, 53 (note 172).

Close study of this table shows that the contents thus catalogued form an organized and structured unity. The structured unity thus discovered must be that of the original poem. With the exception of the Typhoeus episode, we must therefore accept as authentic all the major parts of the text as we have it. This conclusion, however, does not guarantee the authenticity of every line and every sub-episode; on the contrary, the discovery of the poem's basic structure provides solid ground from which to attack the delicate problem of identifying the interpolations. These identifications have been made in the text of our translation by setting them in italics.

The poem falls into twelve sections. The first and last sections are sharply separated from the rest and closely interrelated with each other, because in both the emphasis is on Zeus' monarchy and his dispensation to mankind. Thus Hesiod does what he says the Olympian Muses do (line 48): "they honor Zeus both at the beginning and at the end of their song." The intervening sections fall into two groups: the first four sections (II-V) describe the basic structure of the physical and the human cosmos, and the primal conflict in the divine cosmos. The next six sections (VI-XI) show the emergence of Zeus' monarchy from the conflict in the divine cosmos and his reorganization of the divine, the human, and the physical cosmos.

A more complex grouping is suggested by the systematic alternation of emphasis on either the divine, the human, or the physical aspect of the cosmos. If we pursue this suggestion by observing where Hesiod has placed the main breaks in his poem, we find that sharp breaks isolate the first and last sections, while the ten intervening sections fall into five groups of pairs. Sections II and III are bound together by the anticipations of conflict between Sky and his children (lines 137-53); they give the basic features in the physical and the divine cosmos, with emphasis on the theme of conflict in the latter. Sections IV and V are bound together, and separated from both the preceding Section III and the subsequent Section VI, by an abrupt shift from narrative to catalogue style; they describe the basic polarities in the human cosmos and complete the picture of the physical cosmos. Sections VI and VII are linked together as, strictly speaking, anachronistic anticipations of Zeus' new order before he has won his victory: they both describe aspects of Zeus' monarchy which show continuity between Zeus and older powers in the cosmos, thus forming a middle link between the earlier and later parts of the poem; Section VI (Styx) shows the effect of Zeus' relations with older powers on the divine cosmos, while Section VII (Hecate) shows the effect of Zeus' relations with older powers on the human cosmos. In contrast with Sections VI and VII, Sections VIII-XI show discontinuity and conflict between Zeus and the older powers, thus returning, at a higher level and on a larger scale, to the theme of conflict in the divine cosmos first established in Sections II-III. And in Sections VIII-XI Hesiod systematically alternates his emphasis from description of the conflict in the divine cosmos to description of the consequences of the conflict for the human cosmos: in Section IX (Prometheus) the emphasis is on the fateful consequences for mankind, and in Section XI (Tartarus) it is on the functioning of Night, Day, Sleep, and Death in the human cosmos. In Section XII the catalogue of Zeus' consorts and offspring is so organized as to be a fitting capstone to the thematic structure of the whole poem: by his union with Metis (lines 886-900) and the birth of Athena (lines 924-6) Zeus finally resolves the problem of conflict in the divine cosmos; his other offspring impose order on the polarities in the human cosmos.

Hesiod's compositional technique, which is still close to Homer's and to the tradition of oral composition, does not make the relationship of parts to each other and to the whole explicit in the manner to which the modern reader is accustomed; hence the poem has the superficial appearance of being loose and amorphous.[4] But the basic design has a monumental simplicity and grandeur; it is, if anything, formalistic to the

---

[4] Cf. J. A. Notopoulos, "Continuity and Interconnexion in Homeric Oral Composition," in *Transactions and Proceedings of the American Philological Association*, 82 (1951), 81-101.

point of stiffness. There is a geometric pattern reminiscent of the geometric style in early Greek art, a style which is roughly contemporaneous with Hesiod.

II. THE MEANING OF THE *THEOGONY*

Hesiod lived in an age innocent of philosophy. He presupposes an audience familiar with the idiom of mythical thinking and accustomed to speculate on the great questions of life in that idiom. We must therefore translate his speculations into our own idiom, which is primarily philosophical. To decipher his meaning completely, we would have to reconstruct, with the aid of historical research and imagination, the entire picture of the world on which he and his audience had been brought up. To grasp the general outline of his thought, it is sufficient to explore the speculative implications of the general structure of the poem as analyzed in the previous discussion.

The key to the speculative structure of the *Theogony* is the idea of history; in Hesiod's view, the present order of the universe can only be understood as the outcome of a process of growth and change. Hesiod expresses this idea by the special way he exploits a traditional mythological form—that of the genealogical catalogue.

First, by systematically extending the traditional mythical genealogies till everything significant in the physical, the divine, and the human cosmos is included, and by then deriving this totality from two primal powers, Void and Earth, Hesiod establishes a pattern of progressive differentiation. This progressive differentiation is represented in Hesiod's mythical language as a process of proliferation stimulated by an immanent creative energy which Hesiod calls Desire: that is why Hesiod enthrones Desire as one of his primordial cosmic powers, side by side with Void and Earth. Secondly, by grouping his genealogical material into four generations, Hesiod establishes a pattern of successive eras, each of which has left a mark on the cosmos. The physical cosmos was not completed in a day or a week: the broad outlines—Earth, Sky, Mountains, Sea—were laid in the first generation, but the details—Rivers, Sun, Moon, Dawn, Winds, Stars—were not filled in till the third generation. The human cosmos, which in the second generation received the accursed children of Night and the blessed children of Sea, is altered in the third generation by the interventions of Hecate, Prometheus, and Zeus, and is not complete till the fourth generation. The divine cosmos is supplied with successive rulers by each of the first three generations, and its personnel is not complete till the fourth generation.

The process of evolutionary proliferation is given a specific direction by the emphasis Hesiod places on the principle of authority in the universe and on the sequence of rulers who exercise authority. In a detailed and elaborate narrative style, matched elsewhere only in the story of Prometheus, Hesiod tells how the first patriarch Sky imprisoned his children until his son Cronus castrated him, how Cronus swallowed his children until his son Zeus escaped, and how Zeus defeated the Titans in battle and became King. The sequence of Sky—Cronus—Zeus is the main line through Hesiod's genealogical ramifications, and it is a line with a definite beginning and a definite end. Zeus is the end-term; the conviction that the cosmic historical process culminates and terminates in the monarchy of Zeus is stamped on the whole structure of the *Theogony*. The beginning-term in the sequence of rulers is Sky, but the beginning-term in the procession of Being is Earth; not only the line of rulers, but, in fact, the whole realm of Being is descended from Earth. Of the three primal powers—Void, Earth, Desire—Desire has no offspring, and Void, which is a sort of personified "nothingness," produces nothing positive: Void produces the distinction between Darkness and Light and between Night and Day (Section II), and later in the poem (Section IV) Night is the parent of a number of destructive forces in the human cosmos.[1] Not only is Earth the great Mother of all, but also her first batch of offspring, including

---

[1] See the analytical table on page 12, to which constant reference is made in the following pages.

her future mates Sky and Sea, are produced by her parthenogenetically.

Earth and Zeus are the alpha and omega, the beginning and
the end, of Hesiod's cosmic history. The contrast between the
two shows the direction of the cosmic evolution. Earth and the
first generation that she produces parthenogenetically—Sky,
Mountains, Sea—are essentially physical; they are deified aspects of nature. Zeus and the Olympians are essentially anthropocentric; they are deified aspects of the life of man. In between come the Titans. Of the twelve Titans, only one (Ocean)
has a name signifying a nature-personification, but five of
them (Ocean, Tethys, Hyperion, Thea, Crius) produce offspring which are essentially physical (rivers, heavenly bodies,
winds); the other seven (Cronus, Rhea, Coeus, Phoebe, Iapetus,
Themis, Mnemosyne) produce offspring which are in one way
or another symbolic of the regime of Zeus. Thus the cosmos
has evolved from a natural to an anthropocentric order. Hesiod
repeats this progression in the descendants of Void; Void's
offspring—Darkness and Night—and Night's first offspring—
Light and Day—operate in the physical cosmos, while Night's
second offspring are destructive forces operating in the human
cosmos.

The direction of the cosmic evolution is not only from a
natural to an anthropocentric order, but also from the primacy
of the female to the primacy of the male. This idea is contained in the contrast between Mother Earth at the beginning,
who produces children without male partnership and mates
with her own sons, and Zeus "the father of gods and men"
at the end. In between these two terms, and symbolizing a
transitional stage, we have the recurrent theme of the sub-
version of the authority of the father by an alliance between
the mother and the youngest son: Earth instigates Cronus
to castrate his father Sky, and Rhea saves Zeus from being
swallowed by his father Cronus. In the first instance the
role of the mother is much more important than in the
second instance. In the first conflict Cronus is a subordinate
who executes the will of his mother Earth; Zeus, on the

other hand, while owing his escape to his mother Rhea, goes on to win power by virtue of his own intelligence and strength in the battle against the Titans. Not only is Rhea's role more limited, but the way she performs it is much weaker. Rhea is at her wits' end to save her youngest child and has to turn to her parents Earth and Sky; not only do they formulate the plan, but the execution of it is taken over by Earth: it is Earth who hides the infant Zeus, fools Cronus with a stone, and tricks him into vomiting up the children he had swallowed. The initiative falls on Earth, the primal female power, because of the weakness of her successor Rhea. Thus the total picture is one of a graduated increase in masculine authority. Patriarchal power is finally consolidated when Zeus, faced with the same threat as Sky and Cronus, swallows the potentially dangerous consort Metis and produces her potentially dangerous offspring Athena out of his own head.

Two other myths in the *Theogony*—the birth of Aphrodite and the story of Prometheus—develop the theme of male dominance in the human cosmos under the dispensation of Zeus. In the story of Prometheus, Zeus takes vengeance on mankind for Prometheus' theft of fire by inflicting on them the curse of womankind. Why are women such a curse? The denunciation of the sex with which the section concludes (lines 591-603) emphasizes above all else their economic unproductivity; they are useless drones,[2] a luxury item in a poor man's budget. In Hesiod's world, that is to say, under the dispensation of Zeus, economic production is in the hands of men; in other words, the economy of the human cosmos under the dispensation of Zeus is patriarchal. The attributes with which Hesiod characterizes the prototype of womankind manufactured by order of Zeus are those which are appropriate to women in a culture dominated by males. She is described as girlish and "tender"—the Greek word *aidoios* applies to persons who are protected only by the sentiment of pity inspired by their helplessness—her only hold on men is her irresistible

---

[2] The Greeks knew that bees (i.e., workers) were female and drones male. Hesiod is merely using "drone" as an example of laziness, regardless of sex.

sex appeal (in Hesiod's vocabulary "trickery") based on beauty and personal adornment. Aphrodite, who "presides over the whispers and smiles and deceits which girls employ, and the sweet delight and tenderness of love" (lines 205-06), is the divine counterpart of the prototype of womankind manufactured by Zeus; hence she is given the same attributes of girlishness, tenderness and sex appeal (lines 191, 194, 201-06), and by the same token she is in sharp contrast with Earth, the self-sufficient, dominant female figure in the preceding episode. Aphrodite's affinity with the prototype of womankind and the contrast between her and Earth show that she is the divine symbol of the relation between the sexes in a cosmos dominated by males. It is in this context that Hesiod tells with emphatic elaboration the myth of her birth from the sexual organs of Sky which Cronus cut off and threw into the sea (lines 188-206). To be born thus from the father, not the mother, means, in the language of myth, dependence on or subordination to the father; the birth of Athena from the head of Zeus has precisely the same significance. Birth from the male sexual organs specifies the nature of that subordination: it is the sexual subordination of the female, symbolized by Aphrodite, to the male. And since Earth's revolt against Sky led not to matriarchy but rather, through the intermediate rule of her son Cronus, to the ultimate consolidation of patriarchy under Zeus, it is appropriate that the castration of the first victim of female revolt against male authority should produce the symbol of female dependence, Aphrodite.

The regime of Zeus, which is the final outcome of the historical process, is not only patriarchal, but also political. Zeus is not only "the father of gods and men," but also "the king." Sky is a patriarch pure and simple, exercising despotic rights over his wife and children. Cronus, a patriarch in his dealings with his wife and children, nevertheless seems to go a step beyond the patriarchate when we find some sort of coalition of Titans arrayed against Zeus and the Olympians. Zeus, on the other hand, is elected king by an assembly of the gods after the battle against the Titans. Zeus' position of leadership is not based on kinship but on political alliances: before the decisive battle he invited all the gods to rally to his banner, enticing them with promises of political appointments; his invitation was accepted by Styx, who belongs to the Titan family, and thus Zeus secured her children Glory, Victory, Power, and Strength (Section VI). After being elected king, Zeus' first act is to distribute "honors and offices" to his partisans (line 885).

As king, Zeus has at his disposal force and violence on a scale which puts the petty despotisms of his predecessors completely in the shade. In the battle against the Titans he deploys a battery of force which dominates the whole universe: when he finally lets loose with the lightning-bolts, "the whole earth and the ocean-streams and the barren sea began to boil" (lines 695-6). It is also characteristic of Zeus' reign that his military power is not based on personal strength but on politics. This idea, which is succinctly expressed in the story of how Zeus acquired the children of Styx, is elaborated in the battle against the Titans: the decisive factors in Zeus' victory are the lightning-bolts, manufactured by the Cyclopes, and the support of the Hundred-Arms; the Cyclopes and Hundred-Arms are "forces" which Zeus acquires by releasing them from the prison in which they had been placed by their father Sky. By these political deals Zeus secures the instruments of organized violence which are characteristic of political power: an armament industry (the Cyclopes), and a mercenary army (the Hundred-Arms); after his victory he also establishes an underground prison for his Titan captives and converts his mercenaries into gaolers.

Since Zeus' power is based on politics, his distinctive attribute is not strength but statesmanship—the quality which Hesiod calls *metis*, "Cunning," or "Wisdom," though the word cannot be satisfactorily translated. All authority involves some degree of wisdom: Sky possesses secret knowledge, even after his deposition, as is shown by the oracles which he gives to Cronus, Rhea, and Zeus himself; Cronus, according to the stock epithet applied to him, is a "cunning trickster"; but Zeus surpasses them both when he first marries and then swallows the personification of cunning and wisdom, Metis herself (lines 886-90). Zeus' *metis,* his intellectual supremacy, is shown in action in his struggle against Prometheus (Section IX). Like Cronus, Prometheus is described as a "cunning trickster," but he is defeated by Zeus, who is "full of immortal wisdom"—the moral of the story being that "it is not possible to deceive the mind of Zeus" (line 613). The story of Prometheus is juxtaposed with the battle against the Titans, in which Zeus' power is shown in action; together the two events show that neither force nor fraud can challenge the supremacy of Zeus.

The political character of Zeus' regime explains why he succeeded in establishing a stable regime while Sky and Cronus failed. Sky and Cronus both get involved in a fatal conflict with their children. The cause of the conflict is not explicitly defined in the case of Sky, but we are told that Cronus knew that his own son was destined to supplant him. Both Sky and Cronus try to forestall a possible revolt on the part of their children by violent repression; but this violent repression only provokes the mother into an alliance with the children, and this alliance, by a combination of force and fraud, defeats the father. Hesiod takes pains to emphasize that the fate of Sky and that of Cronus are interconnected by the principle of retaliatory or retributive justice. Earth justifies the attack on Sky on the ground that "he was the one who started using violence" (line 166), and the first episode ends with an anticipatory allusion to the second: "Father Sky called his children *the Titans* . . . he said that they "tightened" (*titainontas*) the noose and had done a monstrous thing for which they would have to pay in time to come" (lines 207-10). Again drops of blood from Sky fall on Earth and cause her to produce the Spirits of Vengeance (line 185), and Rhea, when she turns against Cronus, invokes the Spirits of Vengeance of her father Sky (line 472). Indeed the detailed parallelism between the two episodes is intended to exemplify the retributive principle of an eye for an eye and a tooth for a tooth. Why does Zeus not get engulfed in a fatal conflict with his children? Why does

Zeus not pay for his attack on his father? We cannot say that the law of retribution does not apply to Zeus because his hands were clean, although this position is maintained by certain sentimental interpreters who apparently want to find in Zeus a god who satisfies the demands of their own moral consciousness.[3] To forestall a potential conflict with his children, Zeus swallowed his first consort Metis, thus outdoing Cronus, who had swallowed only the children. Nor is Zeus' armed rebellion and subsequent imprisonment of the Titans—including presumably his father Cronus—any more or any less reprehensible in itself than the rebellion of the Titans against their father. The reason why Zeus escapes the fate of Sky and Cronus is not because he commits no "evil deeds," but because he puts himself beyond good and evil and beyond the reach of the law of retribution. The state, which, like Zeus, inaugurates a new regime of Law, Order, Justice, and Peace for its subjects, is not itself subject to Law. Zeus is the founder of what Machiavelli calls "civil society" in the cosmos, and the best comment on the morality of Zeus is Machiavelli's comment on the morality of Romulus, founder of the Roman state:

. . . many will perhaps consider it an evil example that the founder of a civil society, as Romulus was, should first have killed his brother, and then have consented to the death of Titus Tatius, who had been elected to share the royal authority with him; from which it might be concluded that the citizens, according to the example of their prince, might, from ambition and the desire to rule, destroy those who attempt to oppose their authority. This opinion would be correct, if we do not take into consideration the object which Romulus had in view in committing that homicide. But we must assume, as a general rule, that it never or rarely happens that a republic or monarchy is well constituted, or its old institutions entirely reformed, unless it is done by only one individual; it is even necessary that he whose mind has conceived such a constitution should be alone in carrying it into effect. A sagacious legislator of a republic, therefore, whose object is to promote the public good and not his private interests, and who prefers his country to his own successors, should concentrate all au-

---

[3] For example, Solmsen, *op. cit.,* 25.

thority in himself; and a wise mind will never censure any one for having employed any extraordinary means for the purpose of establishing a kingdom or constituting a republic. It is well that, when the act accuses him, the result should excuse him; and when the result is good, as in the case of Romulus, it will always absolve him from blame. For he is to be reprehended who commits violence for the purpose of destroying, and not he who employs it for beneficent purposes.[4]

Zeus, like his predecessors, commits violence to establish his rule; he continues to use violence to repress opponents of his rule, such as the defeated Titans, Prometheus and his brothers; but unlike his predecessors, he does not suppress his children. In giving birth to Athena out of his own head, he finds a way to release safely even the potentially dangerous offspring of his first consort Metis. Proliferation is a natural law, violated by Sky and Cronus when they attempt to suppress their children; they left their children no choice except to fight in order to exist, and thus involved themselves in a retributory cycle of violence. Zeus, on the other hand, proliferates without conflict between generations, and with unparalleled fecundity. His mates include not only goddesses of his own generation, born of Cronus and Rhea, but also goddesses of the older Titan generation: Metis, Themis, Mnemosyne, Eurynome, Leto—the potentialities of the cosmos remain latent till Zeus actualizes them.

Zeus' regime thus makes a sharp break with the unnatural repression of the past and inaugurates a new order which permits natural development; it is, as the Greek philosophers say, "in accordance with nature." Hesiod expresses this thought in mythical language by the role which he attributes in the *Theogony* as a whole to the primal nature-personifications, Earth and Sky, especially Earth. It is the revolt of Earth against the despotism of Sky which sets in motion the whole process culminating in the supremacy of Zeus. Thereafter Earth and Sky appear as oracles who have foreknowledge of the outcome of the whole process, as a predestined pattern (lines 475-6,

4 Niccolò Machiavelli, *The Prince and the Discourses* (New York, "Modern Library," 1940), 138-39.

891-4); they, especially Earth, take the side of Zeus against his father Cronus (lines 626, 884). When for the first time they take the side of the father and tell Zeus how to handle his first consort Metis, we know that the evolutionary process has come to an end (lines 891-3).

Hesiod lays particular stress on the manner in which Zeus solves the problem of force and violence by finding an outlet for it, thus harnessing for his own purposes the very thing that had caused the downfall of his predecessors. The Cyclopes and the Hundred-Arms are both symbols of the monstrous violence in the cosmos: both of them have freakish physical traits which makes them monsters; both of them are psychologically char-acterized as "violent" or "unruly"; and both of them possess an accumulation of force. These monstrous forms of violence were brought into the world by the first patriarchal authority, Sky; but Sky can do nothing with his own unruly offspring except repress them by shutting them up in the bowels of their mother Earth, thus setting in motion the cycle of retaliatory violence that leads to the downfall of both himself and his son Cronus. Zeus releases them, controls them, and finds a func-tion for them. Thus the force and violence in the universe, which an earlier generation created and then tried to repress, finds a controlled outlet in the political organization of Zeus.

Zeus absorbs into his organization the pre-existing reserves of force and violence—the Cyclopes and Hundred-Arms from the second generation, and the children of Styx from the third. In addition, the catalogue of his children, which celebrates his new creations in the cosmos, includes one figure who symbolizes Zeus' new solution to the problem of force and violence. After the series of unions with goddesses, "Zeus himself produced out of his own head the bright-eyed Tritonian goddess, the terrible queen who loves the clash of wars and battles, who stirs up the fury and leads the armies, never retreating" (lines 924-26). If Athena had been born in a normal way from the mother who conceived her, Zeus' first consort Metis, she would have been a threat to Zeus. By producing her himself, after swallowing Metis, Zeus releases the terrible queen of battle in a manner which dramatizes her affinity with her father and her subordination to him. And Athena is appropriately born from his head, just as the contrasting figure of Aphrodite is appropriately born from the sexual organs of Sky. Zeus' power, as we have seen, is based not on personal strength but on intellectual pre-eminence. The idea that Zeus' power is a product of his wisdom is expressed first by making Metis the mother of Athena, and then by making her be born from Zeus' head.

Machiavelli's principle that the Prince should be judged by the results of his rule rather than by the means used to acquire it, translated into the language of myth, means that Zeus is to be judged in the last resort by the character of his offspring. The catalogue of Zeus' marriages and children, with which the *Theogony* concludes, is in effect a description of the new order —all the more effective because of its restrained formality. This new order of Olympian divinities is, as we said before, anthropocentric. Zeus adds nothing to the physical cosmos; his new divine cosmos is essentially a new order imposed on the human cosmos, and must be judged as such. This new order for the human cosmos can be called civil society, or political organization. It is presided over by King Zeus, who, as Hesiod tells us in the introductory section, also establishes kings on earth (line 96). The introductory section adds that the primary function of kings is to uphold justice: in the catalogue Zeus' second mate is Themis (Law), and his first children are the Hours, Good Order, Justice, and Peace; with these are associated the Fates, whose function is to distribute rewards and punishments among mankind as decreed by King Zeus (lines 901-6). Just as the introductory section placed side by side the bard and the king, two pillars of civilization, so in the catalogue Zeus produces the patron-goddesses of leisure, enjoyment, and artistic recreation, the Graces—Pageantry, Happiness, Festivity—and the Muses (lines 907-9, 915-7). These personifications, together with the terrible queen of battle Athena, form the most striking group in the catalogue: civil society means to Hesiod the reign of law, the arts, and war. Civil society also means a new religion; Hesiod includes traditional gods of Greek religion in the beautiful anthropomorphic form into which they had been transmuted by poetry, especially Homeric poetry. Zeus' new order brings beauty into the divine cosmos: "Next Leto lay with Zeus the lord of the aegis and gave birth to the loveliest pair of children in the whole line descended from Father Sky, Apollo and Artemis the huntress" (lines 918-20). Finally Hesiod turns from Zeus' unions with goddesses and takes up his unions, first, with the nymph Maia and, then, with two mortal women, Semele and Alcmene; Semele, through her union with Zeus, and Alcmene's son Heracles, through his labors, attain immortality (lines 940-55). Zeus' last best gift is to throw down a ladder uniting the human and the divine cosmos and producing a new and higher type of man, the hero.

If this catalogue of Zeus' offspring was a complete description of Zeus' dispensation to mankind, we would have to say that Hesiod looked at the work of Zeus and saw that it was mostly good—not unequivocally good, for Hesiod is realistic and never forgets the force and violence on which Zeus' rule is based: the Fates deal out punishments as well as rewards, and closest to Zeus of all his children, "the equal of her father in power and wisdom," is Athena, "the terrible queen who loves the clash of wars and battles" and who is as important in Zeus' dispensation as her sister Peace. Nevertheless in the catalogue as a whole the shadows are less prominent than the sunlight—the Hours, the Graces, the Muses, beautiful Persephone, the lovely children of Leto, and the crowning mercy of the hero.

It is, however, a mistake to take the catalogue of Zeus' offspring as a complete description of the human cosmos under the dispensation of Zeus. It is a fundamental law of Hesiod's mythical structure that divinities cannot die; they can at most be condemned to impotence, as happens to the Titans when they are imprisoned and to Prometheus when he "lies helplessly bound by a great chain." Zeus' function is not only to create new powers, but also to reorganize the old. We have seen how he combines both functions in order to achieve a solution to the problem of force and violence. But the human cosmos has received a legacy not only from the fourth generation (Zeus' children), but also from the second and the third. A complete description of the human cosmos under Zeus must take account of this inheritance from the past and of Zeus' disposition of it.

The catalogue of Zeus' children suggests that in the human cosmos there is darkness as well as light, terror as well as beauty. This polarity is developed with tremendous emphasis in the section which Hesiod devotes to describing the fundamental nature of the human cosmos (Section IV). Hesiod starts off with a long, grim catalogue of the descendants of Night, who all represent destructive forces at work in the human cosmos, arranged in groups clustering around the key figures of Death, Vengeance, Deceit, and Strife (lines 211-32). In immediate juxtaposition and in the sharpest possible contrast there follows the beautiful catalogue of the Nereids, the fifty daughters of Nereus, the eldest son of Sea (lines 240-64). All but four of the Nereids are given allegorically significant names, so that the total effect of the catalogue is to give a picture of the sea and its role in the life of man. Altogether they form a group of gracious influences in the human cosmos, for their names include groups which signify beauty, generosity, leadership, and success. Thus Hesiod exploits the traditional catalogue form to express his personal philosophy; the mere juxtaposition of the descendants of Night with the daughters of Nereus is sufficient to establish a polar tension as the foundation of the human cosmos. Hesiod then goes on to trace the descendants of the other children of Sea, Thaumas, Phorcys, and Ceto. These are children of Sea and Earth; in contrast with Nereus, the offspring of Sea alone, they introduce a note of wonder and terror. The key figures are Thaumas, whose name means "wonder," and Ceto, whose name means "monster." Thus the polarity in the forces permeating the human cosmos is expressed not only in the contrast between the Night family and the Nereus branch of the Sea family, but also in the contrast between the two branches of the Sea family;

for Sea has not only a beneficent side, but also a darker side. And even the darker side has a sort of terrible beauty in it: the marvels and monsters include the Harpies, "whose streaming hair is so beautiful," the Graiae, whose faces are beautiful and who are always finely dressed, and Medusa, who slept with Poseidon on a bed of springtime flowers (lines 267-79).

The polarity, which achieves its most emphatic expression in the contrast between Night and Nereus, runs like a continuous thread through every stage of the cosmic process. The contrast between Night and Nereus repeats the contrast between the two primal powers from which they are descended— Void and Earth: the polarity in the human cosmos is derived from a polarity in the physical cosmos; at no point in the *Theogony* is there any intermarriage between the descendants of the two primal powers. Then again Earth and Sky produce two contrasting types of children: on the one hand the Titans, the parents of order in the physical, divine, and human cosmos, and on the other hand the Cyclopes and Hundred-Arms, who are symbols of disorder and violence. Even in the powers which issue from the severed organs of Sky there is a contrast between the Spirits of Vengeance and the Giants—symbols of violence again—and the tender and beautiful goddess Aphrodite.

The human cosmos receives its first legacy from Night and Sea (Section IV); it receives its last increment from Zeus (Section XII); it also receives a legacy from the intermediate generation of the Titans, primarily through Hecate (Section VII) and Prometheus (Section IX). Here again the same polarity is apparent. Hecate and Prometheus are both powers that mediate between mankind and the gods: Hecate has "a share in the rights and privileges of each and every one of the gods," and "men on earth call on Hecate whenever they wish to make propitiation" (lines 415-22); Prometheus champions mankind against the gods in his division of the sacrificial meat and in his theft of fire. But whereas Hecate operates with the consent of Zeus and altogether beneficially, Prometheus attempts to operate against Zeus and with disastrous results; for with the blessing of fire came the curse of womankind. Not only is the polarity bequeathed to the human cosmos by Night and Sea repeated in the legacy of the Titan generation, but there are analogies between the two levels so that the second is reminiscent of the first. The catalogue of benefactions conferred by Hecate shows her to be a goddess who combines in her own one person the attributes of the fifty daughters of Nereus: she has generous gifts; she gives victory and success; she promotes political leadership; she helps "men who work on the dark and treacherous sea." Prometheus, on the other hand, "the cunning trickster" who "quarreled with the purposes of the all-powerful son of Cronus," embodies some of the most pernicious forces among the descendants of Night: Deceit, Strife, Lawlessness, and Madness.

What difference does the advent of Zeus make to the polarity in the human cosmos? His relations with the older powers and his new creations both show that while Zeus strengthens the forces of good in the human cosmos, the underlying polarity is not abolished but is even intensified.

Zeus strengthens the forces of good by absorbing the old ones into his dispensation. The description of Hecate, the great and good intermediary between mankind and the gods, emphasizes that Zeus not only left her privileges intact but also added to them. Hesiod combines Hecate with Leto. Leto's outstanding characteristic is said to be gentleness and kindness toward men and gods, and, though belonging to the Titan generation, she is a recognized member of the Olympian hierarchy (lines 407-08); in Section XII we are told that Zeus mated with her and produced the loveliest pair of gods, Apollo and Artemis (lines 918-20). But perhaps the most striking illustration of the absorption of the forces of good into the dispensation of Zeus is the catalogue of the daughters of Ocean, the Oceanids (lines 346-70). The catalogue of Oceanids duplicates the catalogue of the Nereids; like the latter it is composed of allegorically significant names, which refer either to features of the sea or to favorable influences in the life of man, such as wealth, statesmanship, and success. The affinity between the two lists is emphasized by the appearance of the same names in both, and by the fact that Doris, the mother of the Nereids, is herself an Oceanid. Why then did Hesiod include both these catalogues? The difference between them lies in the fact that the Oceanids are specifically related to the dispensation of Zeus: "the daughters of Tethys and Ocean are the holy race of nymphs who, with the help of Lord Apollo and of their brothers the Rivers, bring young boys to manhood; that is the office which Zeus has assigned to them" (lines 346-48). Not only do the Oceanids obtain a function in the dispensation of Zeus, but they also supply him with two of his consorts—Metis, the mother of Athena, and Eurynome, the mother of the Graces. Thus the Oceanids form a link between the Nereids and Zeus, showing how Zeus finds a place for this type of benevolent influence in his dispensation.

Zeus not only absorbs the forces of good into his own dispensation, but also completes them by adding new creations which fully actualize their potentialities. The catalogue of Zeus' offspring repeats and carries to their logical development tendencies already inherent in the catalogue of the Nereids and the Oceanids. A certain dim religious light surrounds these gracious figures, so that it is not always clear what specific benefits they confer on mankind; nevertheless, through the mists of mythology there emerge three recognizable areas of human culture in which Zeus brings to maturity seeds of progress contained in the Nereids and Oceanids. First, Zeus actualized the potentialities of Law. The catalogues of the Nereids and Oceanids show the existence of law-enforcing tendencies in the universe. They include Metis (Wisdom), Idyia (Knowing), Nemertes (Unerring), Polynoe (Richness of Mind), Autonoe (Independence of Mind), Protomedea (First in Leadership), Leagora (Assembler of the People), Euagora (Good Assembler), Peitho (Persuasion), Themisto (Law). These are the qualities which, according to the introductory section, enable the king to dispense justice (lines 85-90). Zeus' union with Themis (Law), with its double issue of the law-enforcing Hours and the retributory Fates, signifies the establishment of the supremacy of law based on the union of law with force.

Secondly, Zeus has actualized the potentialities of art. The catalogue of the Nereids includes Erato (Lovely), which is also the name of one of the Muses; the catalogue of the Oceanids includes Urania (Heavenly), which is also the name of one of the Muses, and Eurynome, the mother of the Graces. Zeus' union with Eurynome and with Mnemosyne, the mother of the Muses, results in the establishment of festive occasions which promote art (the Graces) and in the differentiation of various types of art (the nine Muses). Thirdly, Zeus brings to final perfection the religion of beauty. The Nereids as a group "inspire many hearts with love," and individually they and the Oceanids are described as "lovely," "desirable," "graceful," "rosy," "crowned with beauty," "with lovely figure and perfect form." Beauty in divinity reaches its highest development in the "loveliest pair of children in the whole line descended from Father Sky" (line 919)—Zeus' children, Apollo and Artemis.

Zeus not only strengthens the forces of good, but also represses some of the forces of evil. While Hecate, the good mediator between mankind and the gods, is absorbed into Zeus' regime, Prometheus, the bad mediator, "lies helplessly bound by a great chain"; and Prometheus' brothers—"lawless" Menoetius and "violent-spirited" Atlas—are similarly repressed (lines 514-20, 616). Zeus assigns his own sons on earth, the heroes, to combat some of the terrible monsters descended from Phorcys and Ceto (lines 280-90); through such labors Heracles attained immortality (lines 950-5).

Nevertheless, in spite of all these signs of progress in the human cosmos, the underlying polarity is not abolished. The children of Night are never annihilated or suppressed; they are still abroad in the world, so that even under the dispensation of Zeus "the earth is full of evils, and the sea is also full," as Hesiod says in his other poem, the *Works and Days* (line 101). The introductory section of the *Theogony*, which contains a concrete picture of the human cosmos in Hesiod's own experience, shows us a world permeated by a conflict between polar forces of good and evil: the function of the king is to stop "feuds"; the function of the bard is to provide relief from sorrow (lines 81-103)—sorrow and feuds are both descendants of Night (lines 214, 227-9).

Sinister powers not only continue to be active under the regime of Zeus, but also are absorbed, side by side with benignant powers, into the new dispensation. The gloomy realm of Tartarus is as much part of Zeus' new order as the bright Olympian pantheon; Hesiod juxtaposes the two (Section XI and XII) and explicitly records the installation of Night and her children Death and Sleep in Tartarus. We have already spoken of how those monstrous symbols of violence, the Cyclopes and the Hundred-Arms, find a place in the new order as mercenaries and gaolers. The same idea is expressed in the story of the flying horse Pegasus, one of the monstrous descendants of Ceto, who now "lives in the halls of Zeus and is the one who carries the thunder and lightning for the almighty lord of wisdom" (lines 285-86). Thus while Zeus' sons, the heroes, are busy combatting monsters on earth, while Perseus cuts off the head of Pegasus' mother Medusa, Zeus finds a place for some of the same breed in his own entourage. Therefore it is only logical that Zeus, who crowned the benevolent powers which he absorbed into his dispensation with new benevolent creations, should also procreate forces fundamentally akin to the sinister family of Night. The retributive Fates, who are listed as the daughters of Zeus' union with Themis (Law), also figure in the catalogue of the children of Night; and Zeus' daughter Athena, "the terrible queen who loves the clash of wars and battles, who stirs up strife and leads the armies and never retreats," has an undeniable affinity with those children of Night called Strife, Wars, Battles, and Slaughters.

This summation of the results of Zeus' administrative reorganization shows that the ambivalent mixture of good and evil in the lot of mankind is carried over from the primal legacy of Night and Nereus into the dispensation of Zeus. In fact, since it is Zeus' function to coordinate all the forces in the universe, the ambivalence in the human cosmos, projected first into a contrast between antithetical powers (Night and Nereus), appears under the monarchy of Zeus as an ambivalence in the role of the monarch himself, for both Peace and the Queen of Battles are his daughters.

This ambivalence in the lot of mankind under the rule of Zeus and in the role of Zeus himself is dramatized in the myth of Prometheus (lines 507-616). The significant results of Prometheus' intervention in the destiny of mankind are (1) Zeus' withdrawal of the gift of fire, (2) Prometheus' bestowal of fire despite Zeus' ban, and (3) Zeus' consequent imposition of the curse of womankind. In other words, the blessing of fire is poisoned with the curse of womankind; the gifts of the gods under the dispensation of Zeus are ambivalent. As to whether Zeus or Prometheus is responsible for the catastrophe, Hesiod seems to be deliberately ambiguous. On the one hand, Prometheus is the original troublemaker: he poisons the dispute between mankind and the gods over the division of the sacrificial animal by a resort to trickery; there is also a suggestion that if Prometheus' brother Epimetheus had not been such a fool as to accept the gift of woman, the disaster might have been avoided (lines 513-15). On the other hand, the decision to visit the sins of Prometheus on mankind belongs to Zeus; Hesiod insists that the whole outcome was planned by Zeus from the beginning (lines 551-52); and it is impossible to read statements like "in his heart he was already planning bad luck for mankind" (lines 551-52), and "how deadly and how irresistible was the temptation with which Zeus was going to catch mankind" (line 589), without attributing malignity to Zeus.

In the context of the *Theogony* as a whole, Prometheus is implicitly contrasted with two other champions of the welfare of mankind, Hecate and Heracles. The same Zeus who turns the efforts of Prometheus into a disaster for mankind confirms Hecate's position as a great mediator between mankind and the gods, able to confer prosperity and success in every line of human endeavor (lines 411-49). The contrast between the abortive mediation of Prometheus and the legitimate

mediation of Hecate emphasizes the fact that the regime of
Zeus changes the relation between men and gods. Prometheus'
intervention in the destiny of mankind begins "when gods and
men came to Mecone to settle their dispute" over the division
of the sacrificial animal (lines 535-36); at this point men and
gods intermingle on a basis of equality. The wrath of Zeus
against mankind is provoked by Prometheus' resort to trickery
in the division of the sacrificial animal, that is to say, by his
attempt to settle the issue between men and gods as if it were
an issue between men and other men. But men and Zeus are in-
commensurable. The conclusion of the story is that "it is not
possible to deceive the mind of Zeus or escape his judgment"
(line 613). In Hecate, on the other hand, Zeus vouchsafes to his
faithful subjects a channel of grace which is opened only at
the discretion of the deity; the description of Hecate emphasizes that access to her is obtainable only through prayer (lines
419, 441) and "by making the sacrificial offerings which the
law commands" (line 417), and that her favors are granted at
her own discretion (lines 419, 429, 430, 432, 442-43, 446). The
regime of Zeus changes the relation between men and gods
from equality to subjection. Hesiod elaborates this idea in the
myth of the Five Ages in the *Works and Days* (109-15): the
Golden Generation "who were in Cronus' time, when he was
King in heaven, lived like gods, with hearts free from grief,
without toil and without sorrow."

The same Zeus, who in the myth of Prometheus indicates the
transcendent superiority of deity over humanity, continues to
mingle on a footing of equality with a special class of men, the
heroes. It is on this note that the *Theogony* ends: we hear how
Zeus slept with the daughters of heroic families; how some of
the women thus honored by the gods were made immortal by
Zeus; how the greatest of all the heroes, Heracles, the son of
Zeus and the mortal woman Alcmene, was after his arduous
labors given a goddess for his wife and "now lives with the
immortals, where neither sorrow nor old age can ever come to
him" (lines 954-55). Heracles and the heroes of whom he is the
archetype not only continue to see the gods face to face, as did

all mankind before the fateful quarrel between Zeus and Prometheus, but also can obtain exemption from the miseries which afflict average humanity: sorrows and old age are two of the children of Night, which make the earth full of evils and the sea also full, but now they do not come to Heracles. In contrast with the heroes, it is the lower classes, "men who earn their bread by work" (line 512)—that part of humanity to whom Hesiod addressed his other poem, the *Works and Days*—which suffer along with their champion Prometheus. Hesiod points out that women are a curse only for poor men: poor men work like busy bees while their wives consume like unproductive drones (lines 593-99). Thus the regime of Zeus establishes inequality not only between men and gods, but also between man and man.[5]

III. THE ORIGINALITY OF THE *THEOGONY*

The *Theogony*, like all mythical poetry, is a reinterpretation of traditional myths in order to create a set of symbols which give meaning to life as experienced by the poet and his age. Hesiod says as much in his own way in his introductory invocation of the Muses. He tells us how the Muses once appeared to the shepherd Hesiod and told him what to sing. This claim to divine inspiration is not a mere literary artifice. "The word of the Muses" came to the shepherd Hesiod just as "the word of Jehovah" came to the herdsman of Tekoa. The poet is a prophet of religious truth, and Hesiod is conscious that the truth revealed to him conflicts with much that passed as truth in his own day: the Muses tell him that they "know how to tell many falsehoods that seem real," as well as to "utter truth" when they wish to (lines 26-27). The *Theogony* is, therefore, not an encyclopedia of orthodoxy—there is no orthodoxy in Greek religion anyway—but the result of a creative reinterpretation which reorganizes old myths, alters them, and supplements them with new inventions.

---

[5] Cf. P. Philippson, "Genealogie als mythische Form; Studien zur Theogonie des Hesiod," in *Symbolae Osloenses*, Fasciculus Suppletus VI (1936), 33.

Hesiod obtained the mythology which he has incorporated into the *Theogony* from three main sources: first, the literature of Homeric poetry; secondly, the unwritten local and tribal traditions of the Greeks; and, thirdly (though this is questioned by some authorities), the mythological literature of the Ancient Near East. In spite of the gaps in our knowledge of all three of these sources we can find in one or other of them the basis of practically every major episode in the *Theogony*. In Homer, Hesiod found the names, parentage, and attributes of the Olympian gods; he also found such major ideas as the organization of the pantheon under the monarchy of Zeus and the relegation of Cronus and the Titans to the underworld.[1] Greek popular traditions included the notions of the primal mother Earth, the fire-stealing culture-hero Prometheus, the magically potent intermediary Hecate, and the concealment of the infant Zeus in Crete.[2] Oriental (Hittite and Canaanite) mythological literature provides parallels so close to Cronus' castration of his own father that, in the absence of satisfactory evidence that this motif was present in early Greek traditions, it seems reasonable to infer that Hesiod somehow obtained it from the East.[3] A detailed analysis of Hesiod's borrowings would be out of place in this introduction; it is enough to indicate that his originality does not consist in free invention.

Hesiod's originality does lie in the selection that he made from the store of motifs available to him and in the organization of his selection into a meaningful structure. He was the first to write a comprehensive and systematic Greek theogony. He may have been stimulated by acquaintance with Oriental literature of similar scope and purpose; judging from the analogy of primitive peoples, Greek popular traditions must have included some cosmological lore. Yet Herodotus' judg-

---

[1] Cf. Solmsen, *op. cit.*, 5-21.

[2] Cf. Kern, *Die Religion der Griechen*, I, 244-72.

[3] Cf. H. G. Güterbock, "The Hittite Version of the Hurrian Kumarbi Myths: Oriental Forerunners of Hesiod," *American Journal of Archaeology*, 52 (1948), 123-34.

ment *(Histories,* II, 53) is still valid: "Hesiod and Homer are the ones who provided the Greeks with a theogony, gave the gods their names, distinguished their attributes and functions, and defined the various types." Hesiod worked the theological lore of the Greeks into a unified pattern, just as the Homeric epic unified their heroic poetry.

Herodotus' judgment also reminds us that Hesiod's pattern secured general acceptance by the Greeks, winning in its own sphere the same nearly canonical authority as the Homeric epic enjoyed. The *Theogony* won acceptance because it presented an interpretation of the cosmos that made sense to the Greeks in terms of their own experience of life. To measure Hesiod's achievement, we must find a point of view which enables us to appreciate the *Theogony* as a response and a contribution to Greek culture.

The best way to get such a perspective is by the comparative method; that is to say, by comparing the *Theogony* with a similar product of another culture. For those who are historically-minded as well as anthropologically-minded, Greek culture is not an isolated phenomenon, but occupies a particular position in history and is definable in terms of its historical relations. The Greeks (along with the Romans and the Hebrews) were pioneers of the early Iron Age; they both built on and broke with the traditions of the Bronze Age, which saw, in the Ancient Near East, the first emergence of urban civilization and higher literate learning (including cosmological literature). Hence comparisons between Greece and the Ancient Near East, where possible, enable us to see the distinctive contributions of the Greeks to civilization. Fortunately for our case there are Ancient Near Eastern texts preserved which in scope and subject matter do bear comparison with Hesiod's *Theogony.* Of these only one is preserved completely enough for the pattern and meaning of the whole to be decipherable. This text is the Akkadian-Babylonian *Creation Epic,* also referred to as the "Babylonian Genesis" or the *Enuma Elish,* from the first two words, meaning "when above." A comparison between the

Theogony and the *Enuma Elish* enables us to see the distinctive quality of the Greek outlook on life and to appreciate Hesiod's achievement in giving expression to it.[4]

The *Enuma Elish* begins "when above" there was no sky, and no firm ground below. The first form of things was water, identified with the primal pair of deities, Apsu (the father of all things) and Tiamat (the mother of all), "their waters commingling as a single body." Then "gods were formed within them": first, another divine pair, Lahmu and Lahamu, who are apparently to be identified with silt formed in the waters; then yet another pair, descended from these but surpassing them, Anshar and Kishar, who are to be identified with the horizon; then Anshar's son Anu (the god of the sky), the equal and rival of his fathers; finally Anu's son Ea (the lord of the earth), who, because of his wisdom and strength, is superior to his father. This brief introductory section gives an evolutionary cosmology, culminating in the emergence of a figure (Ea) who transcends his predecessors by possessing wisdom and understanding as well as strength.

In the first major episode of the *Enuma Elish*, "the brothers," the younger gods, band together and disturb the peaceful repose of Apsu and Tiamat by "surging restlessly back and forth," an act which their parents regard as indecent, insolent, and mutinous. Apsu and his vizier consult with Tiamat; Apsu proposes to destroy the younger gods "that quiet may be restored"; Tiamat recognizes their troublesomeness but favors indulgence; the vizier supports Apsu's original proposal. When the younger gods hear of the plot against them, all are speechless and helpless except the all-wise Ea, who devises an all-powerful magic spell that puts Apsu and his vizier to sleep. When they are asleep he takes the vizier prisoner and kills

---

[4] For a translation of the *Enuma Elish*, see V. B. Pritchard, ed., *Ancient Near Eastern Texts* (Princeton, 1950), 60-72. On the interpretation of the *Enuma Elish*, see H. and H. A. Frankfort, J. A. Wilson, and T. Jacobsen, *The Intellectual Adventure of Ancient Man* (Copyright 1946 by the University of Chicago), 168-174. On the comparison between the *Enuma Elish* and the *Theogony*, see Philippson, "Genealogie als mythische Form," *op cit.*, a pioneer study.

Apsu, after having divested him of his crown and placed it upon his own head. Ea then builds for himself and his divine consort a temple on top of the waters of Apsu, where is born his son Marduk, who surpasses all the gods in both power and wisdom, just as his father Ea had once surpassed all.

In the next major episode, the primal mother Tiamat is incited by the older gods to do battle with the younger gods to avenge the death of Apsu and restore the reign of peace. Tiamat creates all sorts of monsters to lead the attack, finds a second husband called Kingu, makes him captain of her army, and declares him king of the universe. When Ea hears of Tiamat's plot, he consults his grandfather Anshar. Anshar first proposes that Ea attack Tiamat with the same weapons (the magic spell) which had conquered Apsu, but Ea declares these weapons are not adequate to deal with the new enemy. Then Anshar sends his son Anu, Ea's father, representing the combined authority of all the gods, to Tiamat to tell her to cease and desist. But Anu has to return without success. After some deliberation Anshar tells Ea that Marduk, the hero strong in battle, must be sent. Ea sends his son Marduk to Anshar, and Marduk promises to save Anshar and the gods, but on one condition, which is that an assembly of the gods be called to declare him, Marduk, the supreme authority. Anshar summons his parents, Lahmu and Lahamu, and all the gods. The assembly gives Marduk the insignia of royalty, throne and scepter, making him king over the entire universe with supreme authority to command, to exalt or abase, and to punish.

Marduk then sets out against Tiamat, riding the storm-chariot and armed with the weapons of the storm: a bow, lightning, and a net held by the four winds. At his approach, Kingu and his army quail, but Tiamat fights. When Tiamat opens her mouth to swallow him, Marduk sends the winds to hold it open, and then sends an arrow down into her belly and she dies. Tiamat's fleeing army is finally caught in Marduk's net. From Kingu he takes his insignia of power, "the tablets of destinies," and fastens them on his own breast.

Unlike Ea, Marduk does not rest after his victory. He proceeds to organize the physical cosmos. He splits the carcass of Tiamat like a shellfish into two parts: half of it is raised to form the sky and the abode of the high gods; half of it becomes the earth. In the sky he establishes the constellations, the "astral likenesses" of the high gods, to regulate the yearly calendar, also the gates where the sun rises and sets, and the procession of the moon's phases to regulate the months. Then he decides to create man, upon whom the burden of toil will be placed so that the gods can live at ease. Ea fashions man according to Marduk's plans out of the blood of Kingu, condemned as the ringleader in the rebellion. Marduk then organizes the pantheon, stationing three hundred gods to guard the heavens and three hundred to guard the earth.

The gods express their gratitude for their deliverance by building a central temple for Marduk in Babylon, containing subordinate shrines for the rest of the gods. There the gods gather. After a banquet celebration, Anu leads the gods in confirming Marduk's position as king and in celebrating the fifty different names which express his powers, achievements, and functions: he is creator and king of the universe; he saved the universe from destruction; as ruler he dispenses justice and ensures the food supply; he is both a mighty warrior and a mighty magician. On this note the poem ends.

The *Enuma Elish* has been expertly interpreted by Orientalists who also understand the nature of mythopoeic thought. According to Thorkild Jacobsen, the Mesopotamians saw world-order as the result of the organization of the cosmos as a state. In the *Enuma Elish,* Jacobsen writes, "the origin of the world-order is seen in a prolonged conflict between two principles, the forces making for activity and the forces making for inactivity. In this conflict the first victory over inactivity is gained by authority alone; the second, the decisive victory, by authority combined with force. The transition mirrors . . . a historical development from primitive social organization, in which only custom and authority unbacked by force are available to ensure concerted action by the community, to the organization of a real state, in which the ruler commands both authority and force to ensure concerted action." [5] Little comment is needed to show the validity of this analysis. The drama begins when the younger gods assert the principle of movement by "surging restlessly back and forth"; Apsu plots against them to "restore quiet"; Tiamat is incited to rebel so that the older gods can "have rest." Conversely Ea follows up his victory by building a temple, and Marduk follows up his with world-constructing works. The first victory is gained by Ea's wisdom and magic power; for the second victory Marduk is needed, because he adds force and is invested with all the authority of kingship.

In Hesiod, as in the *Enuma Elish,* cosmic history begins with the predominance of powers of nature and ends in the organization of the cosmos as a monarchical state. Both dramatize the violent conflict between old and new in the cosmic process, and explain the cosmic state as growing out of this violent conflict and representing the successful establishment of a monopoly of violence; Zeus, like Marduk, combines authority and force. Both recognize an intermediate stage, itself the result of conflict, between the primeval powers of nature and the final monarchy; Cronus, the cunning trickster, is analogous to the wise magician Ea.

But while Hesiod shares the belief in the all-importance of the cosmic state, he does not share the *Enuma Elish* view of its function. In the *Theogony* the conflict which results in the organization of the cosmic state is not a conflict between the forces of creativity and the forces of inertia. Thus, on the one hand, Zeus does not represent the principle of creativity in the way that Marduk does; he does not, like Marduk, proceed to construct the physical cosmos out of the dead bodies of the forces of inertia, now inert matter in his hands. Nor, on the other hand, is there anything in the *Theogony* that can be called "forces making for inactivity"; on the contrary, the immanent creative energy which Hesiod calls Desire is in all things, driving them to constant proliferation. Hesiod's uni-

[5] Frankfort, Wilson, and Jacobsen, *op. cit.,* 173.

verse is inherently dynamic, and dynamic from the beginning. This inherent dynamism produces by natural proliferation the entire physical cosmos. In the *Enuma Elish* only the limited sequence water-silt-horizon-sky-earth is produced by natural proliferation; from that point on the physical cosmos is constructed artificially by Marduk, that is to say, by state action. Hesiod's universe is not only dynamic, but inherently full of tensions and polarities, which, as we have seen, recur at every level, from the primal polarity between Earth and Void to the final polarities in Zeus himself. This polar structure is quite different from the basic dualism in the *Enuma Elish*, which is then annihilated by the complete victory of Marduk.

For Hesiod, the essential function of state-organization is to establish order in the inherently dynamic and tensioned universe. The universe naturally produces monstrous forms of violence like the Hundred-Arms and chaotic forces like the children of Night. Along with these "problem children" the universe produces forms of authority, in the first place Father Sky, which seek to control them. For Hesiod the central problem is the establishment of an adequate form of authority, and the monarchy of Zeus is his answer. Hence Zeus' role is essentially normative rather than creative as Marduk's; his first creations, through his union with Law, are Good Order, Justice, and Peace. Hence also while Zeus has force, he does not, like Marduk, represent the first emergence of the principle of force; his "forces" are recruited from pre-existing elements of force in the universe. Not force, but wisdom (Metis) is his primary attribute (his first consort); and this wisdom is not the same as the magical knowledge of Ea, but rather a normative insight which gives him "knowledge of good and evil" (line 900).

Since for Hesiod the cosmic problem is to find the right form of authority, the conflict is not, as in the *Enuma Elish*, between authority and chaos but between different forms of authority; while Marduk and Ea form one bloc against the primal pair, the conflict between their opposite members in the *Theogony*, Zeus and Cronus, is the climax of the cosmic drama. Hence, in the first place, Hesiod gives us a more profoundly historical concept of cosmic process; instead of the eternal and static conflict between activity and inactivity in the *Enuma Elish,* we find that the cosmic process generates new conflicts. Hesiod is driven by his own logic even to speculate on the possibility of the overthrow of Zeus (lines 886-900). In the second place, Hesiod's contrast between the inadequate patriarchal authority of Sky and Cronus and the superior political order of Zeus leads him to formulate a problem in the nature of state-organization which is beyond the ken of the Mesopotamian outlook. The patriarchal authority of Sky and Cronus is condemned as repressive; Zeus' political order permits the creative potentialities of the universe to actualize themselves. Thus while the *Enuma Elish* sees only creativity in state-organization, Hesiod sees also its repressive side and demands an order which permits free development.

An order which permits free development is one which does not do violence to the principle of creativity. For Hesiod the conflict is not between creativity and inertia, but between creativity and order. He has a recurring pattern of conflict, to which there is no analogy in the *Enuma Elish,* between the female creative principle, allied with the offspring of her own creativity, and the male principle of authority. Zeus' political order resolves this conflict and is therefore reconciled with the creative principle: Mother Earth, who had helped Cronus to overthrow Sky and Zeus to overthrow Cronus, helps Zeus to eliminate the threat of his own overthrow. Thus while in the *Enuma Elish* the primal powers of nature have to be killed before they can be incorporated into the new order, Hesiod demands a reconciliation between nature and the state; he demands the kind of a state that is "according to nature." Nor does Zeus abolish the tensioned polarities with which the universe is inherently full; on the contrary, they are absorbed, in a sublimated form, into his new order. Zeus' order is like Heraclitus' subtle "hidden" harmony, which is a "harmony in contrariety."

Hesiod's cosmology reflects a more independent and critical

frame of mind than the *Enuma Elish*. Zeus has neither Marduk's absolute power nor Marduk's arbitrary freedom; Marduk
does not operate, as Zeus does, in the shadow of fate and neces-
sity, which bind him to establish a certain kind of order under
pain of being overthrown like his predecessors. Hesiod is free
to make an evaluation of the regime of Zeus, and his evaluation, as we have seen, is critical and realistic enough to recognize the shadows as well as the light. By contrast, the catalogue
of Marduk's names with which the *Enuma Elish* concludes
expresses the uncritical adulation of slaves.

Hesiod critically evaluates Zeus' regime from the point of
view of its effect on man. The slavish adulation of Marduk in
the *Enuma Elish* is no accident. As Thorkild Jacobsen points
out, the position of man in the Mesopotamian cosmic state
precisely paralleled that of the slave in the human state.[6]
Marduk makes man out of the dead body of the guilty ringleader in the rebellion of the primeval forces of chaos, just
as Mesopotamian states integrated troublesome barbarian
tribes into their new order by converting them into "living
tools"; man's destiny is to toil so that the gods can live without
toil. In the human cosmos which Hesiod describes man is no
slave. Man, wherever he came from (Hesiod curiously omits
to tell us his origin), was not created by Zeus for his own purposes, but exists in his own right. Nor does Zeus, like Marduk,
immediately confront man with a monolithic concentration of
demonic power. Zeus' power, though supreme, is necessarily
remote, since he is essentially only the ultimate coordinator
of a plurality of powers not of his own making. Man is immediately confronted with a plurality of demonic powers which
solicit his allegiance: the Muses, the Hours, the children of
Night, the Nereids, Hecate, Prometheus, etc. Hesiod's description of the human cosmos leaves an overwhelming impression
of a rich variety of possibilities in human life, between which
man is free to choose. Man is even free, as the story of
Prometheus shows, to align himself with forces opposed to

---

6 *Ibid.*, 149.

Zeus. Indeed, the fundamental fact of human life under the regime of Zeus is that it has set itself up against Zeus and as a result has suffered a Fall. The notion of a Fall, elaborated in the myths of Pandora and of the Five Ages in the *Works and Days,* sums up the ambiguities of man's position in Hesiod's universe; it also reaffirms the ambiguity in Hesiod's attitude toward the regime of Zeus: the golden age of Cronus, when men lived "like gods, without toil and without sorrow" (*Works and Days,* 112-3), was, at least from one point of view, better.

The Orientalist experts have appreciated the *Enuma Elish* as a response and a contribution to ancient Mesopotamian culture. The great achievement of the Bronze Age in Mesopotamia was, of course, the establishment of cities and civic organization where before there had been only villages and communal organization. As Frankfort says, "the modest life of the prehistoric villager had fitted well enough into the natural surroundings, but the city was a questionable institution, at variance rather than in keeping with the natural order." [7] The maintenance of the new institution of the city demanded a constant struggle with the forces of nature, especially, through drainage and irrigation works, with the watery element. This struggle with nature was cooperative effort, so well organized that Frankfort labels the result a "planned society." [8] The nucleus of this organization was the temple; the myth sustaining the organization was the myth that not only the temple but also the city and its people were both ruled and owned by a god. If we discount some features in the *Enuma Elish* that correspond to the later imperialist phase in the Bronze Age and to the Babylonian supremacy in Mesopotamia, we can see how the major themes of the poem—the conflict between creativity and inertia, the conflict between nature and the state, the theocratic notion of the state, the enslavement of man to the state—correspond to the major structural principles in Mesopotamian society. We can also understand how, from the

---

[7] H. Frankfort, *The Birth of Civilization in the Near East* (Bloomington, 1951), 51.

[8] *Ibid.,* 52-59.

third millennium B.C. and for two thousand years, the annual recitation of the *Enuma Elish* on New Year's Day helped to maintain the structure of that society.

The universe, according to the *Theogony*, is dynamic and full of polar tensions. So was Greek society. Definitions of the essence of Greek culture vary depending on the culture with which it is, explicitly or implicitly, contrasted. A historical definition should take as its point of departure the difference between Greek culture, as one specimen of the early Iron Age, from the Bronze Age cultures which preceded it. The Greeks, the pioneers of the early Iron Age, developed a form of civilization in which power was diffused and decentralized, in contrast with the monolithic concentration of power in the Ancient Near East.[9] In economic life, the cheaper technology of iron, a more complete surrender to the system of private property, and (later) the invention of coined money diffused capital and capitalism to small farmers, merchants, and craftsmen. In political life the traditions of primitive tribal democracy were not lost, as in the Ancient Near East, but grew into a republican framework within which social classes, pressure-groups, and individuals competed for power. In cultural life the invention of the alphabet diffused access to literature, which in the Ancient Near East was monopolized by a specialized caste of scribes in the service of the palace or the temple; for the first time it was possible for a farmer, like Hesiod, to be also a poet. This diffusion of power in the Greek city-state set the stage for a more or less permanent state of competition or conflict between individuals and classes, which, as it developed, made rapid mutations in political, economic, and cultural forms inevitable. Thus Greek culture was faced with two characteristic problems: how to find unity in diversity, and how to find a permanent principle in the midst of flux. These later became the classic problems of Greek philosophy; it is Hesiod's achievement to have formulated them first in mythopoeic terms.

---

[9] Cf. V. Gordon Childe, *What Happened in History* (New York, Penguin Books, 1946), Ch. IX: "The Early Iron Age."

Hesiod lived in a very early period of Greek history (around the second half of the eighth century B.C.) when the characteristic trends of Greek culture were just beginning to assert themselves.[10] Our knowledge of his life and times is derived from his other poem, the more personal and almost autobiographical *Works and Days*. In it he attempts to give a practical, ethical, and agricultural guide for perplexed small farmers caught in the complexities and harshnesses of what Hesiod himself calls the Iron Age. "Would that I were not one of the fifth generation of men, but either had died before or been born afterwards. For this is truly an iron generation: men never rest from labor and suffering by day, or from destruction by night; the gods' gift to them will be heavy troubles. And yet even they will have some good mixed with their evils" (*Works and Days*, 174-9). Hesiod in the *Works and Days* describes his own experience of the forces which, in the *Theogony*, he projects into the structure of the cosmos. He gives a quaint but trenchant description of competitive individualism, which he calls "the Strife which is good for men": "She stirs up even good-for-nothings to work. For a man gets the desire to work when he sees his rich neighbor busy ploughing and planting and putting his house in order. Neighbor vies with neighbor in busy pursuit of wealth; potter is angry with potter and craftsman with craftsman; beggar is jealous of beggar, and poet of poet" (*Works and Days*, 20-6). He sees the dissolution of the old patriarchal and familial morality, and in its place the emergence of a war of every man against every man: "The father will not be at one with his children, nor the children with their father, nor guest with his host, nor friend with friend; nor will brother be dear to brother, as it was in days before. Men will dishonor their parents, quarrelling with them and abusing them with bitter words, hardening their hearts and having no fear of the gods. . . . The man who keeps his oath, the just, the good, will get no thanks; but rather evil doing and violence will be praised. Might will be

[10] Cf. A. A. Trever, "The Age of Hesiod," *Classical Philology*, 19 (1924), 157-68.

right and shame will cease to be" (*Works and Days,* 182-93). His social protest against the new aristocracy, the "gift-de-vouring princes" who pervert justice, testifies to the emergence of conflict between classes (*Works and Days,* 202-64). Against all this disorder Hesiod can only appeal to the throne of Zeus: "There is the virgin Justice, the daughter of Zeus, who is honored and revered by the gods who live on Olympus. When any man offends her by slanderous lying, she then sits beside her father Zeus, the son of Cronus, and recounts the wickedness of men, until the people pay for the mad folly of their evil-minded princes who pervert justice and give crooked sentences" (*Works and Days,* 256-62).

Hesiod's vision of the realities of the Iron Age instructed and inspired some of the greatest social thinkers of Greece, such as Solon and Aeschylus.[11] We today are still living in the Iron Age. From Hesiod we can gain insight not only into his life, but also into our own.

In conclusion, the editor must record his indebtedness to Dr. Martin Ostwald of Columbia University for his criticisms of the translation, and to Dr. and Mrs. Thomas Parkinson of the University of California for criticisms of style.

Special acknowledgment is also made to the following publishers for their kind permission to quote copyrighted material in the present volume:

The University of Chicago Press, Chicago, for permission to quote from H. and H. A. Frankfort, J. A. Wilson, and T. Jacobsen: *The Intellectual Adventure of Ancient Man;*

The University of Indiana Press, Bloomington, for permission to quote from H. Frankfort: *The Birth of Civilization in the Near East;*

Random House, Inc., New York, for permission to quote from the Modern Library edition of N. Machiavelli: *The Prince and the Discourses.*

NORMAN O. BROWN

WESLEYAN UNIVERSITY
May, 1953

---

[11] Cf. Solmsen, *op. cit.,* 103-224.

SELECTED BIBLIOGRAPHY [1]

Childe, V. G., *What Happened in History* (New York, Penguin Books, Inc., 1946), pp. 177-97.

Cornford, F. M., *Principium Sapientiae, The Origins of Greek Philosophical Thought* (Cambridge, Cambridge University Press, 1952), pp. 202-49.

Frankfort, H. and H. A., Wilson, J. A., and Jacobsen, T., *The Intellectual Adventure of Ancient Man* (Chicago, 1946), pp. 182-99.

Frankfort, H., *The Birth of Civilization in the Near East* (Bloomington, University of Indiana Press, 1951), pp. 51-9.

Güterbock, H. G., "The Hittite Version of the Hurrian Kumarbi Myths: Oriental Forerunners of Hesiod," in *American Journal of Archaeology*, Vol. LII (1948), pp. 123-34.

Kern, O., *Die Religion der Griechen*, Vol. I (Berlin, Weidmannsche Buchhandlung, 1926), pp. 244-72.

Mazon, P., *Hésiode* (Paris, Societé d'edition "Les Belles Lettres," 1928), pp. 3-30.

Notopoulos, J. A., "Continuity and Interconnexion in Homeric Oral Composition," in *Transactions and Proceedings of the American Philological Association*, Vol. LXXXII (1951), pp. 81-101.

Philippson, P., "Genealogie als mythische Form: Studien zur Theogonie des Hesiod," in *Symbolae Osloenses*, Fasciculus Suppletus VI (1936).

Pritchard, V. B., *Ancient Near Eastern Texts* (Princeton, Princeton University Press, 1950), pp. 60-72.

Rzach, A., "Hesiodos," in Pauly-Wissowa, *Real-Encyclopädie der classischen Altertumswissenschaft*, Vol. VIII (Stuttgart, J. B. Metzler, 1913), pp. 1187-201.

Schwenn, F., *Hesiods Theogonie* (Heidelberg, Carl Winter, 1934).

Solmsen, F., *Hesiod and Aeschylus* (Ithaca, Cornell University Press, 1949), pp. 3-75.

Trever, A. A., "The Age of Hesiod," *Classical Philology*, Vol. XIX (1924), pp. 157-68.

---

[1] A number of the works listed deal only in part with the contents and background of Hesiod's *Theogony*. In these instances the pertinent sections have been indicated by the inclusion of page numbers.

NOTE ON THE TEXT

The following translation of Hesiod's *Theogony* is based on the third edition of A. Rzach, *Hesiodi Carmina* (Teubner, Leipzig, 1913). The present text has been divided into twelve sections by means of bracketed headings giving line references to the Greek text. This was done partly to elucidate the structure of the poem and partly to facilitate identification of particular passages. To distinguish Hesiod's original work from later interpolations, interpolated episodes which violate the coherence of the poem as a whole appear in the text in italics and are indented; interpolated lines which violate the sense of the passage have been relegated to the footnotes. The canons underlying the editor's definition of the original poem and his conception of its structure are explained in the Introduction.

N. O. B.

HESIOD'S THEOGONY

THE THEOGONY

[I, 1-115]

Let us begin our song with the Heliconian Muses, whose home is the high and holy Mount Helicon, who with soft feet dance around the violet spring and the altar of the almighty son of Cronus. After they have washed their smooth skin in the Permessus or in the Hippocrene or in the holy Olmeius, they do their dancing, so beautiful and so lovely, on the very top of Helicon: strong is the movement of their feet. Rising up from there they travel through the night, hidden in a thick cloud, but letting their beautiful voices be heard while they sing of Zeus the lord of the aegis, and Queen Hera of Argos, who walks on golden sandals; and bright-eyed Athena the virgin daughter of Zeus the lord of the aegis; and Phoebus Apollo, and Artemis with her showers of arrows; and Poseidon who both supports the earth and makes it quake; and venerable Themis [Law], and Aphrodite with her sparkling eyes; and Hebe with her golden crown, and beautiful Dione; and Leto, and Iapetus, and the trickster Cronus; and Dawn, and the great Sun-god, and the shining Lady Moon; and Earth, and mighty Ocean, and black Night; and the rest of the sacred race of gods who live forever. These Muses once taught beautiful singing to Hesiod as he was pasturing his lambs at the foot of holy Helicon. The goddesses [1] first addressed me with these words: "Shepherds whose home is in the wilds, you miserable disgraces to your trade, all belly and no hands, we know how to tell many falsehoods that seem real: but we also know how to speak truth when we wish to." This was what the eloquent daughters of mighty Zeus said; they also gave me

---

[1] Omitting line 25, which is interpolated from line 52: "the Olympian Muses, the daughters of Zeus the lord of the aegis."

a staff, a branch of evergreen laurel which they trimmed with marvelous skill. They breathed into me their divine voice, so that I might tell of things to come and things past, and ordered me to sing of the race of the blessed gods who live forever, and always to place the Muses themselves both at the beginning and at the end of my song. But enough of this gossiping.

Now let us begin with the Olympian Muses who sing for their father Zeus and delight his great soul, telling with harmonious voices of things past and present and to come. Sweet song pours from their mouths and never wearies; the house of their father Zeus the Thunderer laughs as the lily-like voice of the goddesses floats through it; the peaks of snowy Olympus and the homes of the gods echo with the sound. They lift their immortal voices to celebrate first the venerable primeval generation of the gods, born from Mother Earth and huge Father Sky,[2] and then the gods who are descended from them and from whom all blessings flow. Secondly, they honor Zeus, the father of gods and men, both at the beginning and at the end of their song, since he is the greatest of the gods and the first in power. Next the Olympian Muses, the daughters of Zeus the lord of the aegis, delight the soul of Zeus on Mount Olympus by singing of mankind and of the mighty Giants. These Muses were born in Pieria to Mnemosyne [Memory], the queen of the hills of Eleuther, after her union with Father Zeus the son of Cronus; their nature is forgetfulness of evil and rest from cares. On nine successive nights did Zeus the lord of wisdom unite with her, going to her sacred bed unknown to the rest of the gods; and when the year was up, as the seasons revolved and the months waned and many days had passed, she gave birth to nine daughters all of one mind, all with spirits dedicated to song, all carefree in their hearts. A little way from the topmost peak of snowy Olympus were they born, and that is where their smooth dancing floor and their beautiful home

---

[2] For the sake of vividness I have translated Gaea (Earth) and Uranus (Sky), in spite of the fact that the original names occur in English literature.

is; near them the Graces and Passion keep festive house.[3] As soon as they were born, this immortal choir went in procession to Olympus, glorying in the beauty of their voice. The dark earth echoed all around as they sang, and under their feet a lovely sound leaped up as they went to their father—their father the king of heaven, the sole possessor of the thunder and the blasting lightning-bolt, who by his power conquered his father Cronus, who in his wisdom assigned to each of the gods their properties and settled their privileges.

Such was the song of the Muses whose home is Olympus—nine daughters of great Zeus: Clio and Euterpe and Thalia and Melpomene; Terpsichore and Erato and Polyhymnia and Urania; also Calliope; [4] Calliope is the most exalted of them all, since it is she who attends on the majesty of kings. Whenever the daughters of great Zeus observe the birth of one of those appointed by Zeus to be kings and decide to honor him, they pour sweet dew upon his tongue, and the words flow like honey from his lips. All the people look up to him as he in judgment gives straight verdicts; with his sure eloquence he knows how to bring even large disputes to a quick end. Kings must have strength of mind for this—that they may secure redress for people who are wronged in the market place, their gentle words winning eager consent. Such a king, as he enters the assembly, receives worship like a god and gentle reverence: he is conspicuous in the assembled multitude. Such is the sacred gift of the Muses to mankind. It is the gift of the Muses and of the archer-god Apollo that makes men on earth singers and musicians; it is the gift of Zeus that makes men kings. Fortunate is the man whom the Muses love: sweet words flow from his lips. If someone has sorrow and is sick at heart and stunned with fresh trouble on his mind, and if a servant of the Muses sings of the glorious deeds of men in former times or of the blessed gods whose home is Olympus, he quickly forgets

---

[3] Omitting lines 65-67: "With lovely voices pouring from their lips as they sing the laws of all things and the sure ways of the immortals, with lovely voices pouring forth."

[4] See the Catalogue of the Muses, Appendix, page 85.

his bad thoughts and no longer remembers his troubles: the gifts of these goddesses instantly divert the mind.

Daughters of Zeus, I greet you; add passion to my song, and tell of the sacred race of gods who are forever, descended from Earth and starry Sky, from dark Night, and from salty Sea. Tell how in the beginning the gods and the earth came into being, as well as the rivers, the limitless sea with its raging surges, the shining stars, and the broad sky above [5]—also how they divided the estate and distributed privileges among themselves, and how they first established themselves in the folds of Mount Olympus. Relate these things to me, Muses whose home is Olympus, from the beginning; tell me which of them first came into being.

[II, 116-153]

First of all, the Void [6] came into being, next broad-bosomed Earth, the solid and eternal home of all,[7] and Eros [Desire], the most beautiful of the immortal gods, who in every man and every god softens the sinews and overpowers the prudent purpose of the mind. Out of Void came Darkness and black Night, and out of Night came Light and Day, her children conceived after union in love with Darkness. Earth first produced starry Sky, equal in size with herself, to cover her on all sides.[8] Next she produced the tall mountains, the pleasant haunts of the gods,[9] and also gave birth to the barren waters, sea with its raging surges—all this without the passion of love. Thereafter she lay with Sky and gave birth to Ocean with its

---

[5] Omitting line 111, which is interpolated from line 46: "Also the gods who are descended from them and from whom all blessings flow."

[6] The Greek word is *Chaos;* but this has a misleading connotation in English.

[7] Omitting lines 118-19: "the immortals who live on the peaks of snowy Olympus, and gloomy Tartarus in a hole underneath the highways of the earth."

[8] Omitting line 128, which is interpolated from line 117: "to be the solid and eternal home of the blessed gods."

[9] Omitting line 130: "the Nymphs who live in the wooded mountains."

deep current, Coeus and Crius and Hyperion and Iapetus; Thea and Rhea and Themis [Law] and Mnemosyne [Memory]; also golden-crowned Phoebe and lovely Tethys. After these came cunning Cronus, the youngest and boldest of her children; and he grew to hate the father who had begotten him.

Earth also gave birth to the violent Cyclopes—Thunderer, Lightner, and bold Flash—who made and gave to Zeus the thunder and the lightning-bolt. They were like the gods in all respects except that a single eye stood in the middle of their foreheads,[10] and their strength and power and skill were in their hands.

There were also born to Earth and Sky three more children, big, strong, and horrible, Cottus and Briareus and Gyes. This unruly brood had a hundred monstrous hands sprouting from their shoulders, and fifty heads on top of their shoulders growing from their sturdy bodies. They had monstrous strength to match their huge size

[III, 154-210]

Of all the children born of Earth and Sky these were the boldest, and their father hated them from the beginning. As each of them was about to be born, Sky would not let them reach the light of day; instead he hid them all away in the bowels of Mother Earth. Sky took pleasure in doing this evil thing. In spite of her enormous size, Earth felt the strain within her and groaned. Finally she thought of an evil and cunning stratagem. She instantly produced a new metal, gray steel, and made a huge sickle. Then she laid the matter before her children; the anguish in her heart made her speak boldly: "My children, you have a savage father; if you will listen to me, we may be able to take vengeance for his evil outrage: he was the one who started using violence."

This was what she said; but all the children were gripped

---

[10] Omitting lines 144-45, which are an interpolation expanding line 143: "and they were named Cyclopes because they had a single round eye set in their foreheads."

by fear, and not one of them spoke a word. Then great Cronus, the cunning trickster, took courage and answered his good mother with these words: "Mother, I am willing to undertake and carry through your plan. I have no respect for our infamous father, since he was the one who started using violence."

This was what he said, and enormous Earth was very pleased. She hid him in ambush and put in his hands the sickle with jagged teeth, and instructed him fully in her plot. Huge Sky came drawing night behind him and desiring to make love; he lay on top of Earth stretched all over her. Then from his ambush his son reached out with his left hand and with his right took the huge sickle with its long jagged teeth and quickly sheared the organs from his own father and threw them away, backward over his shoulder. But that was not the end of them. The drops of blood that spurted from them were all taken in by Mother Earth, and in the course of the revolving years she gave birth to the powerful Erinyes [Spirits of Vengeance] and the huge Giants with shining armor and long spears.[11] As for the organs themselves, for a long time they drifted round the sea just as they were when Cronus cut them off with the steel edge and threw them from the land into the waves of the ocean; then white foam issued from the divine flesh, and in the foam a girl began to grow. First she came near to holy Cythera, then reached Cyprus, the land surrounded by sea. There she stepped out, a goddess, tender and beautiful, and round her slender feet the green grass shot up. She is called Aphrodite by gods and men,[12] because she grew in the *froth,* and also Cytherea, because she came near to Cythera, and the Cyprian, because she was born in watery Cyprus.[13] Eros [Desire] and beautiful Passion were her attend-

---

[11] Omitting line 187: "and the Nymphs who on the limitless earth are called ash-trees."

[12] Omitting line 196: "also the foam-born goddess and Cytherea crowned with beauty."

[13] Omitting line 200: "also the sex-loving, because she appeared from the sexual organs."

ants both at her birth and at her first going to join the family of the gods. The rights and privileges assigned to her from the beginning and recognized by men and gods are these: to preside over the whispers and smiles and tricks which girls employ, and the sweet delight and tenderness of love.

Great Father Sky called his children the Titans, because of his feud with them: he said that they blindly had *tightened* the noose and had done a savage thing for which they would have to pay in time to come.

[IV, 211-336]

Night gave birth to hateful Destruction and the black Specter and Death; she also bore Sleep and the race of Dreams —all these the dark goddess Night bore without sleeping with any male. Next she gave birth to Blame and painful Grief,[14] and also the Fates and the pitiless Specters of Vengeance: [15] it is these goddesses who keep account of the transgressions of men and of gods, and they never let their terrible anger end till they have brought punishment down on the head of the transgressor. Deadly Night also bore Retribution to plague men, then Deceit and Love and accursed Old Age and stubborn Strife.

Hateful Strife gave birth to painful Distress and Distraction and Famine and tearful Sorrow; also Wars and Battles and Murders and Slaughters; also Feuds and Lying Words and Angry Words; also Lawlessness and Madness—two sisters that go together—and the Oath, which, sworn with willful falsehood, brings utter destruction on men.[16]

Sea produced Nereus, who never lies and is always true. He was his eldest child, and is called the Old Man of the Sea

---

[14] Omitting lines 215-16: "and the Hesperian nymphs who guard the beautiful golden apples and the trees which bear that fruit on the further shore of great Ocean."

[15] Omitting lines 218-19, which are interpolated from lines 905-06: "Clotho and Lachesis and Atropus, who distribute good and evil among mankind at birth."

[16] See the Catalogue of the Children of Night, Appendix, page 85.

because he is always right and always gentle; he never forgets
the laws, and is full of just and gentle wisdom. Then in union
with Mother Earth, Sea produced great Thaumas, and heroic
Phorcys, and one daughter with a beautiful face, Ceto [Mon-
ster], and one daughter with a heart of steel, Eurybia.

Nereus and fair-haired Doris, daughter of the pure Ocean-
stream, produced in the barren sea children who were goddesses and who inspired many hearts with love—Ploto and
Eucrante and Sao and Amphitrite; Eudora and Thetis and
Galene and Glauce; Cymothoë and Speo and Thoë and lovely
Halia; Pasithea and Erato and Eunice with her rosy arms;
graceful Melite and Eulimene and Agave; Doto and Proto and
Pherusa and Dynamene; Nesaea and Actaea and Protomedea;
Doris and Panopea and beautiful Galatea; and lovely Hippothoë and Hipponoë with her rosy arms; Cymodoce, who,
along with Cymatolege and shapely Amphitrite, is able to calm
the waves of the dark sea and the blasts of stormy winds;
Cymo and Eïone and Halimede crowned with beauty; also
smiling Glauconome and Pontoporea; Leagora and Euagora
and Laomedea; Polynoë and Autonoë and Lysianassa; Euarne
with her lovely shape and perfect form; graceful Psamathe and
divine Menippe; Neso and Eupompe and Themisto and
Pronoë; also Nemertes, who has the same unerring mind as her
immortal father.[17] These are the fifty daughters of Nereus, and
there is no stain on them or on their father.

Thaumas married Electra, the daughter of the deep Ocean-
stream; she gave birth to flying Iris and to the Harpies, Aëllo
and Ocypete, whose streaming hair is so beautiful, and who, as
they soar above on their speedy wings, are as fast as birds or
gusts of wind.

To Phorcys, Ceto [Monster] bore two daughters whose faces
were beautiful, but whose hair was gray from birth; for that
reason they are called Graiae by the gods and by men on earth
—Pemphredo, always finely dressed, and Enyo, always dressed in
yellow. She also bore the Gorgons, who live on the further

---

[17] See the Catalogue of the Daughters of Nereus, Appendix, page 86.

shore of great Ocean, on the border of Night, where the
Hesperian nymphs raise their thrilling voices; their names are
Sthenno and Euryale and Medusa. Medusa had a cruel fate:
she was mortal while her two sisters were immortal and ageless, and Poseidon, the god with azure locks, slept with her in
a soft meadow, on a bed of springtime flowers. So when
Perseus later cut off her head, out leaped huge Chrysaor and
the horse Pegasus. The horse was named Pegasus because it
was born near the *geysers* of Ocean; Chrysaor took his name
from the golden sword which he held in his hands when he
was born. Pegasus flew away, leaving the earth that feeds the
sheep, and joined the gods; now he lives in the halls of Zeus
and carries the thunder and lightning-bolts for the almighty
lord of wisdom. Chrysaor united with Callirrhoë, great Ocean's
daughter, and became the father of the three-headed monster
Geryon, who fell before the might of Heracles in seabound
Erythea, beside his own shambling cattle—

> on [18] *the day when the hero drove those broad-browed cattle
> away to holy Tiryns, having crossed Ocean's ford to fetch
> them and killed the hound Orthus and the herdsman
> Eurytion in the gloomy cattle-stall on the further shore of
> great Ocean. And in a hollow cave Ceto gave birth to an-
> other monster, this one invincible, with no resemblance
> either to mortal men or to the immortal gods—the savage
> Snake-goddess. She is half a nymph with sparkling eyes and
> a beautiful face, and half a monstrous snake, huge and
> terrible, with mottled skin, who eats flesh raw in the under-
> ground regions of holy earth. There she has a cave in depths
> of hollow rock, far from the immortal gods and mortal men;
> there is the august home which the gods have assigned to
> her. She stands guard in Arimi beneath the ground—the
> grim Snake-goddess, a nymph that cannot die or grow old
> through eternity. They say that Typhaon united with her
> in love, the lawless ruffian with the girl with sparkling eyes;*

[18] In the editor's opinion, lines 291-332 (in italics) are not part of the
original poem.

and she became pregnant with savage children. First, she
gave birth to Orthus, the hound of Geryon; secondly, she
bore the invincible and unspeakable Cerberus, who eats flesh
raw, the brazen-voiced hound of Hddes, relentless and strong
with his fifty heads; thirdly, she bore the grim Hydra of
Lerna which Hera the goddess with white arms fostered to
gratify her implacable hostility to the might of Heracles.
But Heracles, the son of Zeus and the son of Amphitryon,
killed this monster with his pitiless sword, aided by war-
like Iolaus and instructed by Athena, the goddess of plunder.
Yet the Hydra was the mother of the Chimaera, whose breath
was irresistible fire. This creature, huge and terrible, swift-
footed and strong, had three heads, one of a lion with glar-
ing eyes, one of a goat, and one of a fierce dragon-snake;[19]
she was conquered by brave Bellerophon and Pegasus. Yet
she was the mother of the murderous Sphinx, which de-
stroyed the sons of Cadmus. She bore the Sphinx after sub-
mitting to the hound Orthus, also the Nemean lion which
Hera, the noble wife of Zeus, fostered and settled in the hills
of Nemea to plague men; there he lived and preyed on man-
kind, the master of Nemean towns, Tretus and Apesas. Yet
he too succumbed before the might of strong Heracles.

The youngest of all the children that Ceto conceived from
her union with Phorcys was the fierce Dragon which in dark
underground depths guards the golden apples with his huge
coils. This is the number of the descendants of Ceto and
Phorcys.

[V, 337-382]

The sons of Tethys and Ocean were the swirling rivers—
Nile and Alpheus and Eridanus with its deep current; Strymon
and Maeander and the beautiful stream Ister; Phasis and

---

[19] Omitting lines 323-24, which are interpolated from *Iliad* VI, 181-2:
"in forepart a lion, in hinderpart a dragon, and in the middle a goat,
breathing a terrible blast of blazing fire."

Rhesus and silvery Acheloüs; Nessus and Rhodius and Hali-
acmon and Heptaporus; Granicus and Aesepus and divine
Simoïs; Peneus and Hermus and the good stream Caicus;
Sangarius and great Ladon and Parthenius; Euenus and Ar-
descus and divine Scamander.

The daughters of Tethys and Ocean are the holy race of
nymphs who, with the help of Lord Apollo and their brothers
the Rivers, bring young boys to manhood; this is the office
assigned to them by Zeus. Their names are Peitho and Admete
and Ianthe and Electra; Doris and Prymno and divinely beautiful Urania; Hippo and Clymene and Rhodea and Callirrhoë;
Zeuxo and Clytia and Idyia and Pasithoë; Plexaura and
Galaxaura and lovely Dione; Melobosis and Thoë and beautiful Polydora; Cerceïs with her lovely shape and brown-eyed
Pluto; Perseïs and Ianira and Acaste and Xanthe; lovely
Petraea, and Menesto and Europa; Metis and Eurynome and
Telesto dressed in yellow; Chryseïs and Asia and passionate
Calypso; Eudora and Tyche and Amphiro and Ocyrrhoë;
also Styx: of all these the most exalted is Styx.[20] These are
the eldest daughters of Ocean and Tethys. There are many
others; indeed there are three times ten thousand slender-
ankled daughters of Ocean, a family of goddesses scattered far
and wide, watching over the land and the depths of the sea
everywhere. There is also the same number of their brothers,
the sons of Ocean and Lady Tethys, the rivers roaring as they
flow. It would be hard for one poor man to tell all their names;
they are known to the peoples living near them.

Thea submitted to Hyperion's love and gave birth to the
great Sun-god and shining Lady Moon, and Dawn, who
brings light to men on earth as well as to the gods in the wide
sky.

The divine goddess Eurybia united in love with Crius and
gave birth to great Astraeus and Pallas and Perses, who surpassed all in knowledge.

Astraeus and Dawn--god and goddess—lay together in love,

---

20 See the Catalogue of the Children of Ocean, Appendix, page 87.

and Dawn gave birth to the violent winds—Zephyr, who brings
fair weather, Boreas, who opens a path for the storm, and
Notus. After the winds, Dawn gave birth to the stars—the
Morning Star and the shining constellations which are the
diadem of the sky.

[VI, 383-403]

Styx, Ocean's daughter, united with Pallas and gave birth
in her house to Glory and beautiful Victory and Power and
Strength. All these exalted children of hers have their home
and station always close to Zeus; they make no journey unless
he leads the way; they always sit at the side of Zeus, the Lord
of the loud thunder. This was the destiny decided for them
by their mother, the immortal Oceanid Styx, on the day when
Olympian Zeus, who throws the lightning, summoned all the
gods to tall Olympus and told them that whoever fought on
his side against the Titans would not have his privileges taken
away from him, but would keep the same office he had held
before among the gods; to those who had had neither office
nor privilege under Cronus' reign, he promised a just share of
both. Immortal Styx was the first to arrive on Olympus, and,
following the advice of her father, she brought her children
with her. Zeus honored her and gave her special gifts: he
made Styx the name by which the gods swear, and he made
her children partners of his home for all time. In the same
way he fulfilled without exception all the promises he made
to the others. Power and dominion belong to him alone.

[VII, 404-452]

Phoebe received Coeus' passionate embraces; god and goddess united in love, and she conceived and bore Leto, the
goddess with the azure robe—Leto always mild, mild from the
day she was born, the gentlest of all on Olympus, kind to men
and to gods. She also bore Asteria, honored name, whom Perses
took to his great house to be his wedded wife. Asteria con-

ceived and gave birth to Hecate, whom Zeus the son of Cronus exalted above all with honors. He gave her fine gifts: he assigned to her rights both in the earth and in the barren sea,[21] and the immortal gods honor her greatly. To this day men on earth call on Hecate whenever they wish to make propitiation with the rich sacrificial offerings which the law commands. The man whose prayer is favorably received by the goddess acquires great honor and wealth with ease. Such is the power of Hecate; she has a share in the rights and privileges of every one of the gods born of Earth and Sky. Nor did the son of Cronus forcibly deprive her of the properties she had received at the hands of the earlier generation of gods, the Titans; she still retains rights on earth and in the sky and on the sea, as assigned in the beginning by the first division of powers. Nor is her rank diminished because she is the only child of her mother; rather it is increased because Zeus honors her. She greatly aids and blesses her favorites: she sits beside kings in the judgment seat to give them majesty, and in the assembly of the people her favorite is conspicuous. When men put on their armor and make themselves ready for war, which destroys so many, Hecate with her generous aid enables her favorites to win victory and obtain glory. The goddess can if she wishes help and bless a contestant in the games: his strength and vigor win an easy victory and he happily carries home a fine prize and brings honor on his parents.[22] And when men who work on the dark and treacherous sea pray to Hecate and to Poseidon, the god whose mighty blows make the earth quake, the great goddess can easily give them a plentiful catch; or, if she wishes, she can easily take it away from before their eyes. Along with Hermes she has power to make the animals on the farm multiply: if she wishes she can make cattle-herds and flocks of mountain goats and woolly sheep greatly increase or greatly diminish. Thus Hecate, though the only

---

[21] Omitting line 414: "and she also received a share of honor from the starry sky."

[22] Omitting line 439: "she is also good to stand by her favorite horsemen."

child of her mother, is endowed with every privilege which
the gods possess.[23]

[VIII, 453-506]

Rhea submitted to the embraces of Cronus and bore him
children with a glorious destiny: Hestia, Demeter, and Hera,
who walks on golden sandals; Hades, the powerful god whose
home is underground and whose heart is pitiless; Poseidon,
the god whose great blows make the earth quake; and Zeus
the lord of wisdom, the father of gods and men, whose thunder
makes the broad earth tremble. As each of these children came
out of their mother's holy womb onto her knees, great Cronus
swallowed them. His purpose was to prevent the kingship of
the gods from passing to another one of the august descendants
of Sky; he had been told by Earth and starry Sky that he was
destined to be overcome by his own son.[24] For that reason he
kept a sleepless watch and waited for his own children to be
born and then swallowed them. Rhea had no rest from grief;
so, when she was about to give birth to Zeus, the father of
gods and men, she begged her own dear parents, Earth and
starry Sky, to help her contrive a plan whereby she might bear
her child without Cronus' knowing it, and make amends to the
vengeful spirits of her father Sky.[25] Earth and Sky listened to
their daughter and granted her request; they told her what
was destined to happen to King Cronus and to his bold son.
When she was about to give birth to great Zeus, her youngest
child, they sent her to the rich Cretan town of Lyctus. Huge
Mother Earth undertook to nurse and raise the infant in the
broad land of Crete. Dark night was rushing on as Earth ar-

---

[23] Omitting lines 450-52: "And the son of Cronus made her one of these
who bring young boys to manhood, for all those who since then have
come to see the light of all-seeing Dawn. Thus from the beginning she
has brought young boys to manhood, and these are her privileges."

[24] Omitting line 465: "despite his strength, as the will of great Zeus
decreed."

[25] Omitting line 473: "and of her children whom Cronus the great
trickster had swallowed."

rived there carrying him, and Lyctus was the first place where she stopped. She took him and hid him in an inaccessible cave, deep in the bowels of holy earth, in the dense woods of Mount Aegeum. Then she wrapped a huge stone in baby blankets and handed it to the royal son of Sky, who then was king of the gods. He took the stone and swallowed it into his belly—the fool! He did not know that a stone had replaced his son, who survived, unconquered and untroubled, and who was going to overcome him by force and drive him from his office and reign over the gods in his place.

The young prince grew quickly in strength and stature. After years had passed Cronus the great trickster fell victim to the cunning suggestions of Mother Earth and threw up his own children again.[26] The first thing he vomited was the stone, the last thing he had swallowed; Zeus set it up on the highways of the earth in holy Pytho under the slopes of Parnassus, to be a sign and a wonder to mankind thereafter.

Zeus also set free his father's brothers from the cruel chains in which their father Sky had in foolish frenzy bound them. They gratefully remembered his kindness and gave him the thunder and the lightning-bolt and flash, which huge Earth had kept hidden till then. In these weapons Zeus trusts; they make him master over gods and men.

[IX, 507-616]

Iapetus took Clymene, the shapely daughter of Ocean, as his wife and entered her bed. She gave birth to a violent-spirited son called Atlas; she also bore proud-spirited Menoe-tius, and Prometheus the cunning trickster, and the half-wit Epimetheus, who brought bad luck on men who earn their bread by work: he first accepted the artificial woman sent by Zeus. Lawless Menoetius, because of his savage insolence and overbearing boldness, was struck by the smoking thunderbolt of Zeus and sent down to the lower darkness. Atlas was con-

---

[26] Omitting line 496: "succumbing to the stratagems and strength of his own son."

demned to hold up the broad sky at the end of the earth,
facing the place where the Hesperian nymphs raise their thrilling voices; there he stands and holds the sky up with head and
hands that never tire. Such was the fate wise Zeus decreed for
him. Cunning Prometheus he bound with unbreakable and
painful chains and drove a stake through his middle.

*And [27] he turned on him a long-winged eagle, which ate his
immortal liver; by night the liver grew as much again as
the long-winged bird had eaten in the whole day. The bird
was killed by shapely Alcmene's heroic son Heracles, who
delivered the son of Iapetus from his evil plight and released
him from his sufferings, with the consent of Olympian Zeus
the heavenly king, who wanted to raise even higher than
before the fame of Theban-born Heracles over all the pop-
ulous earth. This was his purpose; he exalted his son with
honor, and angry though he was he laid aside his former
feud with Prometheus.*

Such was Prometheus' punishment for having quarreled with
the purposes of the all-powerful son of Cronus. For when gods
and men came to Mecone to settle their dispute, Prometheus
placed before them a huge ox, which he had carefully divided,
intending to play a trick on Zeus. He served the men with
meat and entrails rich in fat placed inside the skin and covered with the stomach of the ox, while he served Zeus with
the bare bones of the ox dressed with a covering of white fat:
this was his cunning trick. Zeus the father of gods and men
spoke to him and said: "Son of Iapetus, second to none in this
noble company, how unfairly you have divided the portions,
my friend." With these words Zeus, full of immortal wisdom,
rebuked him. Cunning Prometheus had not forgotten his skill
at trickery and replied, smiling slightly, "Zeus, noblest and
greatest of the gods who are forever, choose whichever of these
portions your heart prefers." He said this with intent to deceive: but Zeus, whose wisdom is invincible, saw and did not

---

[27] In the editor's opinion, lines 523-33 are not part of the original poem.

fail to see the deception; in his heart he was already planning bad luck for mankind, and his plan was about to be fulfilled. With both hands Zeus took up the white fat. Anger filled his mind and fury pierced his heart when he saw the white bones cunningly concealed underneath. (That is why the race of men on earth burn the white bones of animals as a savory offering on the altars of the gods.) But as for Prometheus, Zeus, the master of the clouds, indignantly addressed him saying, "Son of Iapetus, your mind was always the deepest, my friend, and it now appears that you have lost none of your cunning."

Zeus was angry, and his wisdom is invincible. He never forgot this trick, and in return for it he withheld from the race of men who live and die on earth the all-consuming power of fire. But the bold son of Iapetus tricked him again: he stole the radiant light of all-consuming fire in a hollow stalk. This bit deeper into the heart of Zeus the thunder-god: he was enraged when he saw mankind enjoying the radiant light of fire. In return for the theft of fire he instantly produced a curse to plague mankind. At the orders of the son of Cronus, the famous lame smith-god [Hephaestus] shaped some clay in the image of a tender girl. The bright-eyed goddess Athena dressed and decked her in silvery clothes. A marvelous embroidered veil fell from her head and was held in her hands.[28] Round her head the goddess tied a golden diadem on which the smith-god himself had exercised his skill, to please his father Zeus.[29] When Zeus had completed this beautiful curse to go with the blessing of fire, he displayed the girl in an assembly of the gods and men, all decked out in the finery supplied by the bright-eyed daughter of the lord of hosts. Gods and men were speechless when they saw how deadly and how irresistible was the trick with which Zeus was going to catch mankind.

---

[28] Omitting lines 576-77: "Round her head Pallas Athena placed lovely garlands of fresh flowers from the fields."

[29] Omitting lines 581-84: "and on it he lavished much subtle workmanship, wonderful to see: the many beasts which land or sea preserve were worked into the diadem in many kinds, so that it shone with much beauty; they were wonderfully made, like living things with voices."

This was the origin of the damnable race of women [30]—a plague which men must live with. They have no place where the curse of poverty is; they belong with luxury. Just as bees in their hollow hives support mischievous drones—the bees work busily all day till sunset making the white wax, while the drones sit at home in the shade of the hive and harvest into their bellies the fruits of another's labor—so Zeus the thundergod made women mischievous in their ways and a curse for men: he dispensed a curse to go with a blessing.

Whoever [31] seeks to avoid marriage and the troublesome ways of women, and therefore refuses to marry, finds old age a curse without anyone to tend his years; though he does not lack livelihood while he lives, on his death his kinsmen divide up his estate. As for the man fated to marry, even if he get a good wife well suited to his temper, evil is continually balanced with good in his life; if he should get pestilent children, the grief in his heart and soul is unremitting throughout life: this evil has no cure.

Thus it is not possible to deceive the mind of Zeus or escape his judgment. Even the trickster Prometheus, Iapetus' son, was not able to escape the heavy consequences of his anger. In spite of all his cleverness he lies helplessly bound by a great chain.

[X, 617-735]

The Hundred-Arms—Briareus, Cottus, and Gyes—had been bound fast in chains by their father Sky when he turned against them in fear of their size and shape and overbearing boldness. He made them live underneath the highways of the earth. For a long time they lay in their subterranean dungeon far away at the distant ends of the earth, suffering pain and anguish and grief. But now they were restored to the light by

---

[30] Omitting line 590: "This was the origin of female women."

[31] In the editor's opinion, lines 603-12 are not part of the original poem.

Zeus and the other gods born of the loves of Cronus and fair-haired Rhea. The gods were following the advice of Mother Earth, who revealed all the future to them, prophesying that with the aid of the Hundred-Arms they would win the glorious triumph which they prayed for. For there had been a long war with much suffering on both sides and many bloody battles between the Titan generation of gods and the children of Cronus. The mighty Titans fought from the top of Mount Othrys, while the Olympian gods, from whom all blessings flow, the children of Cronus and fair-haired Rhea, fought from Mount Olympus. For ten full years they had fought without ceasing, so bitterly did they hate each other: there was no truce in the hard-fought struggle, no decision for either side; the fortunes of war were equally balanced. Then the Olympians provided the Hundred-Arms with full equipment, with nectar and ambrosia, the gods' own food, and restored their fighting spirit.[32] Zeus the father of gods and men chose this moment to address his new allies, saying: "You fine sons of Earth and Sky, listen while I tell you what is in my mind. For a long time now there has been warfare every day between the Titan generation of gods and the children of Cronus, to decide which shall be the victors and have the supreme power. Your duty is to employ the great strength of your invincible arms in the stress of battle on our side against the Titans; remember that we have been your good friends, and that you are indebted to our action for your release from the agony of imprisonment and for your return from the dark underworld to the light of day."

That was what Zeus said, and good Cottus replied to him saying: "Sir, you tell us nothing that we did not know. We know that you are first in wisdom, first in knowledge; and you have shown yourself able to save immortal beings from a chilling fate. Son of Cronus, you are our master. Thanks to your decision we have returned to this world from that forlorn dungeon in the dark underworld where we had abandoned all

---

[32] Omitting line 642: "When they had been fed with nectar and delightful ambrosia."

hope. For these reasons we will join the bloody battle against
the Titans and strengthen your side in the fierce struggle with
unflagging energy and loyal hearts."

When they had heard Cottus' speech, the Olympian gods,
from whom all blessings flow, applauded. They became even
more eager for war than before: so on that same day a dismal
battle started in which all the gods, male and female, joined—
the Titans on the one side and on the other the children of
Cronus together with the terrible monsters with their enormous strength, whom Zeus had brought from the lower darkness to the light. Each of them had a hundred arms growing
from their shoulders and fifty heads on top of their shoulders
growing from their sturdy bodies. They grasped massive rocks
in their sturdy hands and took their place in the bitter battle
against the Titans.

On the other side the Titans prudently strengthened their
ranks. Both sides employed all the strength in their hands.
The limitless expanse of the sea echoed terribly; the earth
rumbled loudly, and the broad area of the sky shook and
groaned. Mount Olympus trembled from base to summit as
the immortal beings clashed, and a heavy quaking penetrated
to the gloomy depths of Tartarus—the sharp vibration of in-
numerable feet running and missiles thrown. While the weapons discharged at each other whistled through the air, both
sides shouted loud battle cries as they came together, till the
noise reached the starry sky.

Then Zeus decided to restrain his own power no longer.
A sudden surge of energy filled his spirit, and he exerted all
the strength he had. He advanced through the sky from Olympus sending flash upon flash of continuous lightning. The
bolts of lightning and thunder flew thick and fast from his
powerful arm, forming a solid roll of sacred fire. Fertile tracts
of land all around crackled as they burned, and immense
forests roared in the fire. The whole earth and the Ocean-
streams and the barren sea began to boil. An immense flame
shot up into the atmosphere, so that the hot air enveloped

the Titans, while their eyes, powerful as they were, were blinded by the brilliant flash of the lightning-bolt. The prodigious heat filled the Void. The sight there was to see, and the noise there was to hear, made it seem as if Earth and vast Sky above were colliding. If Earth were being smashed and if Sky were smashing down upon her, the noise would be as great as the noise that arose when the gods met in battle. The winds added to the confusion, whirling dust around together with great Zeus' volleys of thunder and lightning-bolts, and carrying the battle cries and shouts from one side to the other, so that the uproar was deafening. It was a terrible conflict, which revealed the utmost power of the contestants. After many heavy engagements, in which both sides obstinately resisted each other, the battle was finally decided.

Throughout the bitter battle Cottus and Briareus and Gyes were in the forefront. They attacked relentlessly, throwing showers of three hundred stones one after another with all the force of their enormous hands, till they darkened the Titans with a cloud of missiles. Their brute force was stronger than all the valiant efforts of the Titans. They then conducted them under the highways of the earth as far below the ground as the ground is below the sky, and tied them with cruel chains. So far down below the ground is gloomy Tartarus: a bronze anvil falling from the sky would fall nine days and nights, and reach earth on the tenth; a bronze anvil falling from the earth would fall nine days and nights and reach Tartarus on the tenth. Tartarus is surrounded by a bronze moat; three thicknesses of night are spread round its bottleneck, above which the roots of earth and barren sea are planted. In that gloomy underground region the Titans were imprisoned by the decree of Zeus, the master of the clouds. The dismal place lies at the end of the monstrous earth. No exit is open to them: Poseidon made gates of bronze to secure the place; a wall runs all the way round; and the three strong brothers, Gyes, Cottus, and Briareus, now live there—guards on whose loyalty Zeus the lord of the aegis can rely.

[XI, 736-819]

There [33] *dark earth and gloomy Tartarus, barren sea and
starry sky, all have their roots and farthest edges, side by
side in order. It is a dismal gloomy region which even gods
abhor, a yawning gulf such that not even after the completion of a full year would a man entering the gates reach
the floor; he would be cruelly tossed this way and that by
storm after storm—a mystery which terrifies even the gods.
There stands dark Night's grim house, wrapped in leaden
clouds.*

In front of them Iapetus' other son, Atlas, stands motionless,
holding the broad sky up with head and hands that never tire.
At this point Night and Day meet and greet each other as
they cross the great bronze threshold: one of them is entering
and the other is leaving; never does the house contain both
of them together; always one is outside passing over the earth
while the other is inside waiting for the time of her journey
to come. One of them brings light and sight to men on earth,
while the other, covered in a gloomy cloud, is cursed Night,
who holds in her hands Sleep, the brother of Death.

There is the home of dark Night's children, Sleep and
Death, mysterious gods. They never show themselves to the
radiant beams of the Sun, either as he climbs the sky or as he
descends again. One of them passes gently over the earth and
the sea's broad back and is kind to men. The other has a heart
of iron and in his innermost soul is pitiless as bronze: when
he lays his hands on a man, he keeps him; even the gods hate
him.

There, in front, stand the echoing halls of the god of the
underworld, strong Hades with august Persephone, his wife.
A hound guards the front; this pitiless monster has a cruel

---

[33] In the editor's opinion, lines 736-45 are not part of the original poem.

trick: he greets those who enter with friendly tail and ears, but he never lets them leave again; he waits and eats up everyone he catches going out through the gates.[34]

There [35] lives an awful goddess hated by the other gods, Styx, the eldest daughter of the circular Ocean-stream. She lives apart from the other gods in a great house shaded by high rocks, with silver columns all around towering up to the sky. Seldom is a message brought to her over the sea's broad back by Thaumas' daughter, swift-footed Iris. But when strife and contention are stirred up between the gods, and one of those whose home is Olympus tells a lie, then Zeus sends Iris to fetch that upon which the gods take their great oath: from far away Iris brings in a golden vase the famous cold water which drips from a high, steep rock. Deep under the highways of the earth a branch of the sacred stream of Ocean runs through black night; to this branch is assigned one-tenth part: with nine silver streams Ocean coils around the earth and the sea's broad back and falls into the watery waste; that one-tenth part flows out from a rock and is the great scourge of the gods. If any of the gods whose home is the snowy tops of Olympus swears falsely after pouring a libation of this water, he lies prostrate without breathing until the completion of a year: he does not come near the ambrosia and nectar to eat, but lies without breathing and without speaking wrapped in his bed, sunk in an evil trance. And even after he has spent a long year in sickness, another trial harder than the first awaits him: for nine years he is cut off from the gods who are forever; for nine whole years he never joins their council or their feasts; in the tenth year he rejoins the assembly of the gods, whose home is Olympus. Such is the power of the ever-living

---

[34] Omitting line 774, which is interpolated from line 768: "of strong Hades and august Persephone his wife."

[35] In the editor's opinion, lines 775-880 are not part of the original poem.

*water of Styx upon which the gods take their oath, the
primeval water which issues from that rugged ground.*[36]

[XII, 820-1022]

After Zeus had driven the Titans from the sky, monstrous
Earth gave birth to her youngest child Typhoeus, after
being united in love by golden Aphrodite with Tartarus.
Typhoeus is a god of strength: there is force in his active
hands and his feet never tire. A hundred snake heads grew
from the shoulders of this terrible dragon, with black
tongues flickering and fire flashing from the eyes under the
brows of those prodigious heads.*[37] *And in each of those terrible heads there were voices beyond description: they ut-
tered every kind of sound; sometimes they spoke the language of the gods; sometimes they made the bellowing noise
of a proud and raging bull, or the noise of a lion relentless
and strong, or strange noises like dogs; sometimes there was
a hiss, and the high mountains re-echoed. The day of his
birth would have seen the disaster of his becoming the ruler
of men and gods, if their great father had not been quick
to perceive the danger. He thundered hard and strong, so
that Earth and broad Sky above, Sea and Ocean-streams, and
the Tartarus region below the earth, all rumbled with the
awful sound. Great Olympus quaked under the divine feet*

---

[36] Omitting lines 807-19, which reduplicate lines 729-41: "There dark
Earth and gloomy Tartarus, barren Sea and starry Sky, all have their roots
and farthest edges, side by side in order. It is a dismal gloomy region
which even gods abhor. The gates flash light; the bronze threshold is
immovable, since it grows with roots set unbroken in native rock. And in
front, away from all the gods, on the further shore of the dark Void, live
the Titans. And the great allies of Zeus the lord of the crashing thunder,
Cottus and Gyes, have their home on the foundation-floor of Ocean;
Briareus was chosen for his prowess by the god who makes the rumbling
earthquakes to be his son-in-law: he gave him his own daughter Cymopolea
to be his wife."

* [See note 35, p. 75.]

[37] Omitting line 828, which reduplicates line 827: "and fire burned from
all his heads as he glared."

of its royal master as he rose up, and the earth groaned also. The heat from both sides, from the thunder and lightning of Zeus and from the fiery monster,[38] penetrated the violet deep and made the whole earth and sky and sea boil. The clash of those immortal beings made the long waves rage round the shores, round and about, starting a convulsion that would not stop. Trembling seized Hades, king of the dead in the underworld, and the Titans who stood by Cronus and who live at the bottom of Tartarus.[39] When Zeus' energy had risen to the peak, he took his weapons, thunder and lightning and the smoking thunderbolt, and jumped on his antagonist from Olympus and struck. He blasted all those prodigious heads of the terrible monster and dealt him a flogging until he was tamed. Typhoeus fell down crippled, and the monstrous earth groaned underneath. Flame streamed from the once powerful potentate, now struck by lightning, in the dim clefts of the rocky mountain where he fell. Large tracts of the monstrous earth were set on fire by the prodigious heat and melted like tin heated in moulded crucibles by skillful workmen, or like iron, the strongest metal, softened by the heat of fire in some mountain-cleft;[40] even so did the earth melt in the flame of the fire then kindled. Zeus, in the bitterness of his anger, threw him into the abyss of Tartarus.

From Typhoeus are descended the winds whose breath drives the rain, except Notus and Boreas, and Zephyr who brings fair weather: these winds are descended from the gods, and to men they are a great blessing. The other winds blow capriciously on the sea: when they fall on the violet deep they cause an evil storm to rage and bring great misfortune to mankind: blowing differently at different times they scatter ships and destroy sailors; men who meet them

---

[38] Omitting line 846, which reduplicates line 845: "from the scorching winds and from the flaming thunderbolt."

[39] Omitting line 852: "at the ceaseless din and terrible struggle."

[40] Omitting line 866: "melts in the holy ground through the art of Hephaestus."

*on the sea have no defense against their mischief. On land,
with its endless stretches of flowers, they wreck the fine creations of groundling man, filling them with dust and ruinous
disorder.*

When the Olympian gods had brought their struggle to a
successful end and had forcibly vindicated their rights against
the Titans, Mother Earth advised them to invite Zeus, with
his far-sighted ken, to be king and lord over the gods. Zeus in
return distributed rights and privileges among them.

Zeus' first royal consort was Metis [Wisdom], the wisest of
gods and men. But when she was about to give birth to bright-
eyed Athena, he deceived her with specious words and trapped
her by a trick, and swallowed her and kept her in his belly.
He did this at the advice of Earth and starry Sky, so that the
kingship should not pass from Zeus to another of the gods.
For Metis was destined to produce children wise beyond their
station—first, the bright-eyed Tritonian goddess, the equal of
her father in power and prudent understanding, and secondly,
an unruly son, the future king of gods and men. But Zeus
forestalled her and kept her in his belly, where she gives him
knowledge of good and evil.

Zeus' second consort was Themis [Law], and that radiant
lady gave birth to the Hours—Good Order, Justice, and pros-
perous Peace—who hourly attend the labors of mankind, and
to the Fates—Clotho [Spinner], Lachesis [Allotter], and Atropus
[Inflexible]—to whom Zeus gave the great privilege of distrib-
uting good and evil among mankind.

Next Eurynome, Ocean's daughter, whose form inspired
many hearts with love, gave Zeus three daughters with beautiful faces, the Graces—Aglaea [Pageantry], Euphrosyne [Happi-
ness], and lovely Thalia [Festivity].⁴¹

Next Zeus entered the bed of Demeter, the lady who nour-
ishes all life, and she gave birth to Persephone, with her white

⁴¹ Omitting lines 910-11: "From their eyelids and their glance desire
came dropping, to soften sinews; and the glance from their brows is beautiful."

arms, whom Hades, with the permission of Zeus the lord of wisdom took forcibly from her mother.

Next Zeus became enamoured with fair-haired Mnemosyne [Memory], and she produced the nine Muses with their golden diadems, who enjoy festivities and the delights of song.

Next Leto and Zeus, the lord of the aegis, lay together and she gave birth to the loveliest pair of children in the whole line descended from Father Sky—Apollo and Artemis, with her showers of arrows.

Lastly Zeus took Hera as his wife to bear him children. After she had lain with the monarch of gods and men she gave birth to Hebe and Ares and Eileithyia.

Zeus himself produced out of his own head the bright-eyed Tritonian goddess, the terrible queen who loves the clash of wars and battles, who stirs up the fury and leads the armies and never retreats. Hera in turn, in resentment and jealousy, without union with her husband, produced famous Hephaestus, the master craftsman in the line descended from Father Sky.

> To [42] *Amphitrite and the god who makes the earth quake with a mighty rumble was born great Triton. The power of this awful god reaches far: he rules the bottom of the sea, where he lives in a golden palace near his own mother and great father. To Cytherea and Ares, the god who pierces shields, were born Panic and Fear—terrible figures who join their father Ares, the sacker of cities, in the chill of battle and rout disciplined regiments of men—and also Harmonia, whom Cadmus proudly took to wife.*

Zeus' sacred bed was also shared by Maia, Atlas' daughter, who gave birth to noble Hermes, the herald of the gods. Likewise Semele, Cadmus' daughter, lay with him in love and became the mother of a son with a glorious destiny—Dionysus the giver of joy. She was mortal when she bore her immortal son; now they are both immortal. Alcmene also lay with Zeus

---

[42] In the editor's opinion, lines 930-37 are not part of the original poem.

the master of the clouds and gave birth to the strong man Heracles.

Hephaestus,[43] the famous lame smith-god, took Aglaea, the youngest of the Graces, to be his wife and bear him children.

Golden-haired Dionysus took fair Ariadne, the daughter of Minos, as his wife, and the son of Cronus later made her also immortal and ageless. The strong man Heracles, mighty son of shapely Alcmene, after completing his painful labors, was joined in solemn marriage with Hebe, the daughter of great Zeus and Hera who walks on golden sandals, on the snowy mount of Olympus—lucky man! He accomplished his great work and now lives forever with the immortals, where neither sorrow nor old age can touch him.

To [44] the Sun-god, who never wearies, the famous Oceanid Perseïs bore Circe and Aeëtes the king. Aeëtes, son of the Sun-god who shines light for men, was chosen by the gods to be the husband of another daughter of the pure Ocean-stream, Idyia with the beautiful face. Golden Aphrodite made her submit to his love and she bore shapely Medea.

And now farewell, gods whose home is on Olympus; farewell, islands, continents, and salty sea in between. Now sing, you Olympian Muses, daughters of Zeus the lord of the aegis, of the line o; goddesses who, though immortal, lay with mortal men and bore godlike children.

Demeter, the great goddess, united in sweet love with the hero Iasion, in a fallow field ploughed three times, in the fertile land of Crete; she bore Plutus [Wealth], a good spirit who goes everywhere on land and on the sea's broad back, enriching and giving great prosperity to whomever he meets and joins hands with.

To Cadmus, in Thebes crowned with beauty, Harmonia, golden Aphrodite's daughter, bore Ino and Semele and

---

[43] In the editor's opinion, lines 945-46 are not part of the original poem.

[44] In the editor's opinion, lines 956-1022 are not part of the original poem; the original poem ended at line 955.

Agave with the beautiful face; also Autonoë, whom long-haired Aristaeus married, and Polydorus.[45]

To Tithonus, Dawn bore Memnon, the king of the Ethiopians, known by his bronze crest, and also Prince Emathion. And to Cephalus she gave a son with a glorious destiny, strong Phaëthon, a godlike man; while he was still a young child with childish thoughts, in the tender flower of glorious youth, he was snatched by smiling Aphrodite, who flew away with him and made him the divine spirit who is her nocturnal acolyte in her holy temple.

Medea, King Aëtes' daughter, was stolen from Aëtes—so the gods had decreed—by Jason the son of Aeson. After completing the many painful labors imposed on him by great King Pelias, that proud, lawless, savage man of violence, Jason returned to Iolcus after many adventures, bringing that girl with sparkling eyes on his swift ship; there he made her his wife to bear him children. She submitted to Jason, who was like a shepherd to his people, and bore him a son, Medeus, whom Chiron the son of Philyra brought up in the mountains. Thus the will of great Zeus was fulfilled.

Of the daughters of Nereus, the Old Man of the Sea, the divine goddess Psamathe loved Aeacus through golden Aphrodite and bore Phocus; and silver-footed Thetis, also a goddess, submitted to Peleus and bore Achilles, that lionhearted destroyer of men.

Aeneas was born to Cytherea, crowned with beauty, after she had united in sweet love with the hero Anchises on the peaks of Ida with its many wooded folds.

Circe, the daughter of Hyperion's child, the Sun-god, loved Odysseus, famous for his endurance, and bore Agrius and Latinus, the strong man with no stain.[46] This pair rules

---

[45] Omitting lines 979-83, which reduplicate lines 287-90: "Ocean's daughter Callirrhoë was united in love by golden Aphrodite with the bold hero Chrysaor; she gave birth to a son who surpassed all men in strength— Geryon, who fell defending his shambling cattle from the might of Heracles in seabound Erythea."

[46] Omitting line 1014: "She also bore Telegonus through golden Aphrodite."

APPENDIX

Catalogues of the Theogony

CATALOGUES OF THE MUSES
[Lines 76-79]

The names of the Muses express personifications of the different functions which Hesiod attributes to them. Clio means "celebrate," as the Muses are said to do in lines 44 and 67; Euterpe means "delight" (cf. lines 37, 51, 917); Thalia means "festivity" (cf. line 917); Melpomene means "choir" (cf. line 69); Terpsichore means "delight of dancing" (cf. lines 4, 7); Erato means "lovely" (cf. line 70); Polyhymnia means "many songs" (cf. lines 11, 37, 51); Urania means "heavenly" (cf. line 71); Calliope means "beautiful voice" (cf. lines 10, 41, 68).

CATALOGUE OF THE CHILDREN OF THE NIGHT
[Lines 211-232]

At first sight the catalogue of the Night family seems to consist of an indiscriminate heap of unpleasant things in human life: closer study shows that Hesiod has arranged it in well-thought-out groups. The key figure in the first group is Death: Hesiod introduces three synonyms for death to suggest death in all its forms, and adds Sleep and Dreams, on the ground of the affinity between sleep and death. The key notion in the second group is retribution: the most prominent figures in this group are the Fates and the Specters of Vengeance, but Blame (and its by-product, Grief) and Retribution are also mentioned. The final group is introduced by the notion of Deceit; Deceit is followed by Love; the deceitfulness of Love is manifested by its juxtaposition with two things which are in contradiction with it, Old Age and Strife.

Strife is the only one of the children of Night who produces further children of her own. This distinction is due partly to the prominence of Strife in Hesiod's view of the universe, and

partly to the nature of the children of Strife. In contrast with
the children of Night, who represent inevitable limitations
and evils in human life, the offspring of Strife are man-made;
they are the result of human actions inspired with the spirit of
Strife. They, like the children of Night, fall into three groups.
In the first group Strife is presented as causing an interruption
in economic productivity, and consequently bringing Distress,
Famine, and Sorrow. In the second group Strife is presented as
the cause of armed conflict; the third group shows Strife as the
cause of legal disputes and the perversion of justice.

CATALOGUE OF THE DAUGHTERS OF NEREUS
[Lines 240-264]

The names of the Nereids have an allegorical significance
which makes the catalogue meaningful and functional, and
not simply ornamental. The names fall into several groups.
The first is a small group whose name contains the Greek root
meaning "give," do—Doris, Eudora, Doto; the mother of all
these nymphs is also called Doris. This group of names refers
in general terms to the generous bounty of the sea. Another
small group are honorific names appropriate to any group of
nymphs as such: Erato (Lovely), Agave (Illustrious), and
Melite (Honey-sweet). The largest group are names which indicate different aspects of the sea, which was so important a
factor in Greek life: the substance of the sea, as in Cymo
(Wave), Halimede and Halia (Salty); the geography of the sea,
as in Speo (Cave), Nesaea and Neso (Island), Actaea (Shore),
Panopea (Panorama), Eione (Strand), and Psamathe (Sand); the
moods of the sea, as in Galene (Calm), Glauce (gray), Cymothoë
(Running Waves), Hippothoë (Running Horses), Hipponoë
(Temper of Horses), and Menippe (Strength of Horses). An-
other large group refer to the art of sailing: Ploto (Sailing),
Sao (Safety), Thoë (Speed), Eulimene (Good Haven), Kymodoce
(Ready for Waves), Cymatolege (End of Waves), Glauconome
(Mastering the Gray Sea), Pontoporea (Crossing the Sea),
Eupompe (Good Voyage). Another group refer in more general
terms to successful venture: Eucrante (Success), Eunice (Vic-

tory), Proto (First), Pherusa (Carry), Dynamene (Capable). The last group refer more specifically to successful leadership, especially political leadership: Protomedea (First in Leadership), Leagora (Assembler of the People), Euagora (Good Assembler), Laomedea (Leader of the People), Polynoë (Richness of Mind), Lysianassa (Royal Deliverer), Themisto (Law), Pronoë (Forethought), Nemertes (Unerring); this group reflect the qualities which Hesiod attributes to their father Nereus— unerring judgment and respect for justice. There are also included four names which are not allegorical but are simply mythological names of sea-goddesses: Amphitrite, Thetis, Pasithea, Galatea. These different types of names are scattered throughout the catalogue, except that the names referring to political leadership are reserved till the end, while the names at the beginning in general have a more direct connection with the sea. The beauty of the catalogue is based on the effectiveness with which Hesiod exploits a traditional mythical form to express his own content—the role of the sea in the life of man, and the existence of friendly powers in the human cosmos counterbalancing the dismal children of Night. Cf. Introduction pp. 27ff.

CATALOGUE OF THE CHILDREN OF OCEAN
[Lines 346-370]

As in the catalogue of the Nereids, the beneficence of the Oceanids is expressed by including in the list a number of allegorically significant names. Of these the largest group refer to the sea: Callirrhoë (Beautiful Stream), Amphiro (Surrounding Stream), Ocyrhoë (Fast Stream), Plexaura (Goading the Breeze), Galaxaura (Calming the Breeze), Thoë (Fast), Pasithoë (All-fast), Petraea (Rocky). Another group refer to blessings of one kind or another: Doris (Giver), Eudora (Good Giver), Polydora (Generous Giver), Pluto (Wealth), Tyche (Luck), Melobosis (Fruit-growing). A final group refer to qualities of human leadership: Peitho (Persuasion), Idyia (Knowing), Metis (Wisdom), Menestho (Steadfast), Eurynome (Far-ruling), Telesto (Success). Cf. Introduction, pp. 29f.